Factory

D1202463

Objekt

Titles in the *Objekt* series explore a range of types – buildings, products, artefacts – that have captured the imagination of modernist designers, makers and theorists. The objects selected for the series are by no means all modern inventions, but they have in common the fact that they acquired a particular significance in the last 100 years.

Series editors: Joe Kerr and David Crowley

In the same series

Aircraft
David Pascoe

Factory

Gillian Darley

REAKTION BOOKS

Published by Reaktion Books Ltd
79 Farringdon Road
London EC1M 3JU, UK

www.reaktionbooks.co.uk

First published 2003

Printed in Hong Kong

British Library Cataloguing in Publication Data

Darley, Gillian
    Factory. - (Objekt)
    1.Factories - History 2.Factories - Social aspects
    3.Factories - Design and construction
    I.Title
    338.6'5'09

ISBN 1 86189 155 5

Contents

Acknowledgements

My thanks are due to many people who have taken an interest in the subject of the factory and have given me tips and pointers along the way. I met with help and a warm welcome at the Faguswerke, Alfeld, and at Boots, Nottingham, where Alan Brown was an erudite and enthusiastic guide. The following have helped in specific ways: June von Essen, Adrian Forty, Murray Fraser, Eva Jiřicna, Philippa Lewis, David Pascoe, Carole Rifkind, Andrew Saint, Matthew Slocombe, Elina Standertskjold, Robert Thorne, Derek Brampton at the Triangle Bookshop, Ken Worpole and the team at Reaktion Books, in particular my editor, Joe Kerr, who has been engaged but never interfering – an ideal combination of attributes. And, as ever, to Michael and Susannah, a large bouquet for their patience, support and love in a time of distraction.

Preface

Factories, so often inscrutable envelopes of human activity, are intriguing on many levels. Dante was galvanized by the demonic turmoil he found inside the Arsenal in Venice, where 'the gluey pitch they boil in winter/to smear on their leaking boats'[1] made unseaworthy vessels sound again, while alongside in the blackness continued a manufacturing process that, even in Longfellow's fruity Victorian translation of 1867, conveys the orderliness of the medieval mass production line: 'One hammers at the prow, one at the stern, / This one makes oars, and that one cordage twists, / Another mends the mainsail and the mizzen.' As far as I am aware, Canto XXI of the *Inferno* is the first time that a factory enters literature.

My reason for diverting the editors of the new Objekt series from the topic that they originally proposed to me towards this one was its links to two areas that have long interested me and on which I have written widely – utopian and industrial model settlements and functional vernacular buildings. Also, as an architectural assessor and critic, over the years I've visited a fair number of new factories and been struck by how apparently quite modest design or planning decisions can positively transform a complex working environment. A factory can be a dull hut or an inspiring structure – in the widest possible sense.

Factory is built around a series of interconnected essays. I begin by looking at the powerful *imagery* of factories, an apt metaphor for progress and change, a picture both sublime and romantic. The following two chapters trace, chronologically, the potential of the factory as a *model* – social, organizational, architectural or a combination of all three. Industrial buildings should, logically, be *innovators* in materials and systems: from the eighteenth century onwards they have been places where practical solutions have been sought – and reached – and technologies exchanged. At the beginning of the twentieth century, the pull of mass production and a new fascination with the machine and all its works required potent architectural *icons*, a few of which were factories – functionally explicit and extending the apparent possibilities of materials and construction. Some factories, on the other hand, were designed to be advertisements. The relatively short history of the building as *sales* vehicle – part of a larger exercise that is now known as branding – runs from such flights of fancy as the tobacco factory designed like a mosque (for exoticism) to contemporary notions of modernity and chic conveyed in buildings designed by fashionable 'big name' architects. Finally, what of the new factory in the post-industrial age? As manufacturing cities reinvent themselves and transform the remnants of their industrial fabric into magnets for leisure, sport, international conferences, even as places to live, the new campuses of industry have moved to the countryside, often within reach of the nearest university, where the contemporary version of the factory, quiet and self-contained, has become a *laboratory* more likely to be dealing with ideas than heavy metals, places where women and men work on equal terms.

From the eighteenth century onwards, factories have been markers: of revolution, technical and social, of innovation, in design and in process, of their moment, politically and economically.

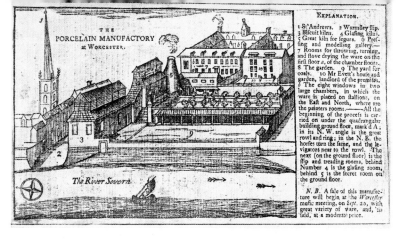

As such, factories are essentially short-lived, reflecting the exact circumstances of time and place with some precision. In the optimistic heyday of the Industrial Revolution the factory could be seen to stand for British mercantile strength and activity, or alternatively for the dark forces of wage-slavery. Friedrich Engels's eye-witness reports from Manchester were the material of Karl Marx's *Das Kapital*. The epitome of change, in itself both threatening and energizing, the factory has provided images as black or

Industry in the 1780s. The porcelain works is shoehorned into the centre of Worcester.

Preston, Lancashire, seen from the outlying countryside in 1831. Industrialization remains confined to the city, and wind and steam power are still in competition.

as white as the argument required. Nor has any single building type better supplied the always evanescent notions of modernity, its radical potential exaggerated far beyond the realizable.

The new factory is a heavy expense on the wrong side of the balance sheet; directors and shareholders will not necessarily see the point of it. Yet, as an architectural commission the factory is a particular kind of challenge – in one observer's words, offering 'leaner meat for architectural thought'. It requires enormous experience and expertise to design successfully a high quality, low-cost building, one that is both flexible and practical for the industrial process as well as being a sympathetic environment for the workforce. By definition, those that appear on these pages carry with them higher than usual aspirations.

An early morning stroll on the Fiat Lingotto test track, looking out over the rooftops of Turin towards the Italian Alps, is as good

The blighted industrial landscape around Charleroi, Belgium, painted by Constantin Meunier in the early 1880s.

a place as any to ponder the unpredictable fate and form of the factory. As a building Lingotto has roots in common with hundreds of Soviet industrial plants built in the 1930s, themselves parented by the massive assembly-line factories built for the automobile manufacturers of Detroit. Until now, Fiat has remained an Italian-owned company, producing cars in the area around Turin, but the Lingotto plant itself became redundant in the mid-1980s and narrowly escaped becoming builders' rubble.

The modern conference delegate, jet-lagged after a lengthy journey across time zones, is probably unaware that his or her smart hotel not far from the piazzas and elegant streets of Turin was once a car factory. The open production floors are now subdivided into hundreds of comfortable hotel rooms, self-contained offices, shops and art facilities, while the internal courtyards have become thickly planted exotic groves.

The executive office 'bubble' and helipad added to the rooftop at Fiat Lingotto, Turin, by the Renzo Piano Workshop in 1999.

Yet, up on the roof, the lengthy test track with its two dizzily cambered turns announces that this building was dedicated to movement, and was celebrated by the architectural avant-garde of the 1920s as no other single building in Europe. The rooftop road-way is now a jogging track for international business folk, shaking off the tensions of the day's meetings with a kilometre or two run at a pace which better suits the tight corners of this odd circuit.

No motor vehicles come this way any more, except from the air. Above the track and balanced like a saucer placed carelessly on the outer edge of a table are the helipad and blue-glass executive office bubble that Renzo Piano, the Italian-born international architect who masterminded this transformation, has added to translate the image of the building and its roots in the Machine Age into the twenty-first century.[2] Today in Turin, industrialists, whose interests probably touch many countries and continents, can alight on the rooftop, stopping just long enough to confer with their fellow directors in the glazed globe teetering above the helipad, before dodging back under the blades and taking off into a wider world.

Then, in the early weeks of 2003, the end of the great auto-mobile oligarchies was epitomized by the death and lying-in-state of Giovanni Agnelli. At Fiat Lingotto an endless file of black-clad mourners packed the spiral ramps and wound out onto the rooftop track to pay their last respects. His stylish, post-industrial resting place was in Renzo Piano's just-completed pavilion, a sleek, angled marker for the art gallery below, itself the latest phase of the transformation of Lingotto.

Change is the only certainty in manufacturing and the fast forward button is permanently engaged. Even in the brief gestation of this book, Dyson has moved its manufacturing base to Asia while General Motors hovers over Fiat. In Britain alone, it has been calculated that 150,000 manufacturing jobs were lost in a single year, 2001–2. No commodity is too commonplace or too luxurious to be made more cheaply elsewhere.

Michigan, the heart of the American 'rust-belt', is currently grafting 'its auto industry roots . . . onto the electronic age'. What the State's Economic Development Corporation calls advanced manufacturing technology is permitting 'a combination of manufacturing, information technology, design and engineering', replacing the serried ranks of heavy manufacturing premises with the lush campuses of biotech and electronics companies. Meanwhile, production of the Rolls-Royce, the last reminder of the days of handmade carriage building, has left Crewe in the industrial north-west of England for a state-of-the-art factory and headquarters built by its new German owners, BMW, in private parkland on the Goodwood estate in West Sussex. A manufacturing history which began in a green and pleasant land has turned full circle. The changes and chances, opportunities and misadventures of the capitalist system make up a continual, unpredictable flux, out of which has emerged an intriguing programme, one that is still very much work in progress.

1 Factory as Image

The man who builds a factory builds a temple.
Calvin Coolidge

Witnessing the extraordinary scenery and weather of the Polar regions, C. J. Sullivan, a young blacksmith on the British Antarctic Expedition of 1839–43, struggled to describe his impressions in a letter home. Faced with sheer mountains of glittering blue-white ice, towering waves and ferocious winds, experiencing absolute terror alongside the wild beauty, he searched for a forceful enough metaphor from his own experience with which to convey the overwhelmingly strange and wonderful scene. It was, he decided, like 'a Steem engine in a large factory'.[1]

By then, steam power had become synonymous with thrusting modernity, technological mastery and social upheaval. It also gave new impetus to the aesthetic concept of the sublime, which had formerly been applied to stormy views of the natural landscape, the elements at their most violent or scenes of turbulent industry. Since the 1750s the Severn Gorge in Shropshire had became the Vesuvius of northern Europe, Coalbrookdale a Vulcan's forge of smelting ovens, huge kilns and blast furnaces spewing smoke and jets of flame, flaring against the night sky, as depicted by the theatrical scene painter Philippe de Loutherbourg and witnessed by thousands of astonished travellers. The arrival of the steam engine added force to Romantic visual imagery and, for those with the imagination, opened up an incredible future. As

The iron works in Coalbrookdale, a souvenir in the form of a print for the numerous visitors to the most famous of all early industrial sites. William Pickett (after Philippe Jacques de Loutherbourg), *Iron Works, Coalbrookdale* (1805).

Matthew Boulton reported to James Watt, everyone was becoming 'STEAM MILL MAD'.

If the engines were fearsome beasts, it was equally essential to deal with the anxiety that surrounded the unknown, to placate these new demons, and the more thoughtful of the early industrialists were careful to adapt the architectural style that best reflected continuity – in their case the Classical style – for the public face of their factories. The early years of the Industrial Revolution were full of both hopes and worries; the short, dramatic history of one mill tells the story.

The opening of the Albion Mill in London in March 1786 was a grand and widely publicized event. Behind its heavy walls, Boulton and Watt, the leaders in heavy engineering and machine design and financial partners with the architect Samuel Wyatt and three others in this enterprise, had installed their latest steam-

Pehr Hilleström's painting of a well-dressed party visiting a steel works in Sweden in the 1780s. The thrill of such scenes attracted many visitors, including foreign industrial spies.

driven rotary engine. It was only the third that the Birmingham company had so far supplied for commercial use.[2] Despite the partners' nervousness about the untested nature of their new engine, they could sense the enormous commercial potential for such a highly visible operation in the centre of the capital. The huge new building and its activities were being carefully scrutinized by its admirers and opponents alike.

At a stroke, the Albion Mill brought the industrial scene of the early 1780s to the heart of London, a titan amidst the hundreds of backyard workshops, belching chimneys and loading wharves along the south bank of the Thames. The handsome mill was designed to grind flour in unprecedented quantities, powered by steam. The new 'Fire Engines', as they were known, threatened a revolution for the 500 or so existing corn mills in the London area that had long depended upon wind or water for their energy. In theory at least, steam-powered milling had the capacity to produce flour on a prodigious scale, each engine working many pairs of stones simultaneously. In addition, the engines could power the sifting and preparation of the flour as well as the ventilation of the building. Working men looked on in horror, fearing the failure of traditional milling and with it their jobs. As a monopoly it threatened higher prices for bread. What none of them knew was that the promoters of the Albion Mill were gambling heavily with a largely untried technology. The confident Classical façade, mimicking the current vogue in public buildings and country mansions, masked a very risky enterprise indeed.

Viewed across the new Blackfriars Bridge, on the Surrey side of the river, the Albion Mill was majestic, well suited to its prominent riverside position at the heart of the city. It floated upon a rusticated base, with a heavy watergate punched through beneath, and then rose five storeys above, with stately Venetian windows to mark the principal bays. Extra light came from a rooftop lantern that illuminated a central stairwell. Behind this display of well-mannered and informed urban architecture was the traditional arrangement of a corn mill, in which the upper storeys served as granaries from which the grain was gravity-fed down to the milling area. The coal was brought by river into a dock. Little of this functional business was given away by the muted neo-Classical elegance of the river frontage.

In such a dominant position, the Albion Mill offered a proud architectural, commercial and mercantile riposte to William Chambers's recently completed Somerset House, a little further up and across the river, replete with government offices and learned and artistic bodies. As both architect and chief promoter, Samuel Wyatt envisaged his handsome mill as a flagship, in an ambitious attempt to draw London south across the Thames, a plan underlined by the residential square that he had already developed alongside.

Behind its polite face, the heavy construction of the Albion Mill relied more upon load-bearing columns and a piled foundation structure of inverted arches, as well as a heavy interior wall that could deal with the weight of the engine beams, than upon its outer shell. Wyatt designed the building with flexibility in mind, should expansion be necessary or even if it should be converted back into warehouses at a future date.

The mill quickly became the industrial wonder of the capital – despite endless difficulties with the untried technology, rising debt due to commercial ineptitude and the continuing pulse of anger from rival millers and working men. Boulton's flair for publicity ensured that it became a fashionable location in which to hold events, masques and balls, and the mill was frequently visited by the more enquiring representatives of the aristocracy and City

The ALBION MILL, *Blackfriars Bridge*?

grandees, such as the Directors of the East India Company and the Bank of England, as well as eminent figures from abroad such as Thomas Jefferson. The technical hitches and financial worries remained well hidden from visitors. Sited directly opposite the western boundaries of the City of London, the Albion Mill (as its name alone inferred) appeared to be a definitive emblem of British industrial eminence.[3]

When the Albion Mill exploded in flames before the eyes of horrified Londoners in March 1791, it was far more than merely just another industrial accident of a kind to which Northern textile mills were proving so prone. The same people who had earlier visited the site and wondered at the novel features of the mill were drawn back to watch the terrible theatre of its dramatic incineration, amplified to horrifying effect in the waters of the Thames. Charred embers, ashes and even husks of corn blew across the city, drifting down over the rooftops of Whitehall itself and giving onlookers all too tangible proof of the event.

Samuel Wyatt's design for the palatial Albion Mill in London on the Surrey bank of the Thames. Barges came and went beneath, passing through the rusticated river arch.

The Albion Mill, its palatial masonry walls and windows silhouetted against the harsh illumination of the wall of fire inside, could have been mistaken for one of the public buildings of the City of London in festive mood, customarily lit with thousands of lamps and transparencies for royal or national celebrations. Brilliant and disintegrating, the mill was a kind of terrible counter-image to such festivities.

Inevitably, rumours began that the fire had been started by machine-breakers, fearing for the loss of their livelihoods, but the answer turned out to lie not with incendiaries or even with inflammable sources of lighting, but with untested technology, pushed beyond its capacity. The young Scot John Rennie, who had been Boulton & Watt's supervising engineer on the Southwark site since 1788, reported back to his employers after the disaster and identified the cause of the fire as an overheated bearing, due to Samuel Wyatt's insistence on over-running the machines. The venture was still not financially sound, and by pushing production to the limit Wyatt had hoped finally to get the enterprise on to a firm footing.

The fire at the Albion Mill spelled enormous financial loss for the promoters, exultation to the millers and their supporters and a pause for reflection for those who had invested their hopes and energies in an industrial future. The fire was also a topic of urgent interest and concern in the coffee houses and drawing rooms of London, as no fire in a distant Pennine textile mill would have been. For a few days, the incident had brought thrilling, horrifying beauty to the city, a glimpse of the sublime to stand comparison with the much admired flaring foundries and furnaces of Coalbrookdale. Even the aesthete Horace Walpole, who until then had been unaware of the existence of the Albion Mill, was moved to ask where the terrible fire had taken place, 'supposing they were powder mills in the country that had blown up'.[4]

Samuel Wyatt had unquestioningly turned to an architectural vocabulary that suited the importance of the site and the function of his building. He well understood the French eighteenth-century idea of *convenance* and matched it with an 'appropriate character'.[5] Many of the first industrialists had similarly reassured themselves, applying the familiar elements of the Palladian style, well known to them from the town halls and country houses of the shires, to the new structures of manufacture. Before that, early eighteenth-century industrial buildings had been generally ad hoc: a wing of a farmhouse might be converted in a rudimentary fashion, a kiln, forge or foundry tucked under a lean-to extension, while out-workers simply used their own cottages, or outhouses and farm buildings, as their workplaces.

Classical architecture reflected the power of the new industrialists. It was also well-mannered, fitting dress for buildings that intruded on some of the most beautiful valleys of northern England. A pediment pierced by a bull's-eye window, a masonry string course, strongly marked quoins or even a handsome Palladian window on the main elevation pointed out the massive new mills as appropriately 'polite' architecture – regardless of the cruder sheds tacked on behind them. At the Etruria pottery at Stoke-on-Trent (see illustration on page 107), even the bottle kilns were ornamented with fascias and blind windows, light touches specifically requested by Josiah Wedgwood and his business partner.

Thus dressed in a seemly fashion, the factory immediately became a feature that could vie with the mansion, church or ruined castle nearby as a suitable subject for artists. One of the earliest 'portraits' of an industrial building was by Joseph Wright of Derby, who in the 1780s painted Richard Arkwright's Cromford cotton mills by night. Wright depicted three close-packed mills,

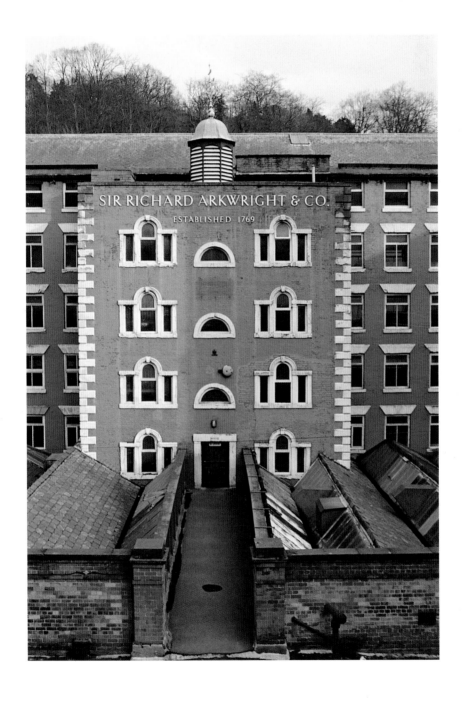

Masson Mills, Cromford in Derbyshire. Built in 1783 and dignified with the details of a neo-Palladian country house.

their seven storeys spectacularly illuminated by tiers of windows and their forms lightly sketched into a steep Derbyshire valley with the help of a bright but veiled moon and back-lit clouds. The image was like a contemporary peep-show transparency, the building back-lit for effect. One admirer of the painting likened the mills to a great man-of-war at sea, dependent on a vast number of men toiling within. Perhaps, more literally, Arkwright's enterprise was comparable to an East Indiaman travelling confidently into unpredictable oceans, many paper fortunes resting on the success of the venture – just as at the Albion Mill.

The epitome of the mill as a Picturesque adjunct to the country house – before long the Cromford mills appeared alongside Chatsworth House on Derby china – was in the landscape architect Humphry Repton's Red Book for Armley House, near Leeds.[6] These books, prepared individually for clients, were an ingenious device of his own invention, in which a watercolour overlaid by

Cotton mills at Cromford, Derbyshire, transformed into a dramatic landscape subject.
Joseph Wright, *Arkwright's Cotton Mills by Night* (c. 1783).

Benjamin Gott's Armley Mill, West Yorkshire, shown as a proud addition to the landscape. Humphry Repton, 'Red Book' (without overlay) for Armley House near Leeds (1810).

A typical Late Victorian mill, marked by its soaring chimney, set in otherwise unchanged pastoral Pennine scenery. Haworth, West Yorkshire.

another on a flap illustrated the scene before and after improvements. Unusually, Repton decided to humour his client, Benjamin
Gott, a leading textile manufacturer and merchant, by featuring
his newest and most advanced factory, Armley Mill, in the 'after'
view in the Red Book of 1810. The prominent mill appears centre
stage, a bulky stone building viewed from the Kirkstall Road as a
pleasing culmination to the vista across the water meadows.
Above and behind it, set into parkland, stands Gott's mansion,
Armley House, proprietorial but somewhat dwarfed, perched on a
slight eminence. Leafing through the Red Book, showing it to a
succession of distinguished visitors from home and abroad, Gott,
the son of a surveyor and engineer, may well have taken more
pride in his innovatory mill than in his country house. He was a
pioneer in the mass production of woollen goods, and his considerable empire included spinning mills, fulling and finishing plants.
As a major supplier of woollen cloth, chiefly blankets, to the
British and allied armies, the Napoleonic Wars were good for Gott.

A woollen mill viewed as an eye-catcher in the landscape was
certainly a novel ornament compared to the more usual false ruin
or castle-fronted farmhouse. Repton also humoured Gott by
including on the horizon the distant smoking chimneys of his
mills in central Leeds. Armley Mill itself, in Repton's words 'an
interesting object by daylight and at night . . . a most splendid
illumination of gas light', was the last word in modernity, following its rebuilding after a serious fire. Five years earlier, Gott had
spent the very considerable sum of £23,508 on it.[7] The new Armley
Mill was the first woollen mill known to be of fireproof construction, heated by steam and lit by gas. Yet this innovatory building
was, Repton continued in his commentary, an honest structure that
'looks like what it is – a Mill and Manufactory . . . not disguised
by Gothic windows or other architectural pretensions'. Repton was

happy to celebrate his client's pride in the building but, on his own account, did not include Armley in any of his publications, preferring to emphasize his work on the parks and estates of the aristocracy and landed gentry.

With its novel features, Armley Mill became immediately famous. When the Prince of Wales and his brother the Duke of Clarence visited Yorkshire in 1806, the duke took a tour of Gott's works but the future king demurred, since 'the smell of the different things used in dyeing etc is apt to make him unwell'.[8] Many, like the prince or Humphry Repton, preferred to distance themselves from this kind of reality. Nevertheless, from the earliest moment, the Industrial Revolution had drawn a tide of admiring visitors and industrial spies from abroad; conversely, since the 1780s British manufacturers, inventors and entrepreneurs had seized the chance to take their ideas abroad and to follow raw materials, labour and markets into northern Europe. With the end of the Napoleonic Wars many more joined the exodus. English industrialists were to be found at the helm of heavy engineering works and textile mills across France, Belgium and northern Germany, while foreign governments were eager to import expertise, in person or on paper.

In the confident years of the early nineteenth century, industrialists had abandoned the Classical dress in which they had shrouded the previous generation of mills and factories and reverted to a more functional and robust building type – more telling of the machinery and processes that they were housing, and of the effort to engineer a fireproof envelope, than of stylistic and typological allusion. Image and reality had fallen into step.

Karl Friedrich Schinkel arrived in 1826 for a tour of British industry. As the leading architect for public works in Prussia, he was eager to see examples of the new technology and materials for himself. His travelling companion, Peter Beuth, was head of the

department of trade and industry and the man charged with discovering what lessons could be learned from British pre-eminence in manufacturing. The pair hurried northwards via the Midlands, hardly glancing at the historic towns and ancient monuments along the way. Schinkel's observant journal emerges as the most vivid and graphic account of industrialized Britain of its period.

Beuth had already been in England in 1823, on a similar mission, when he wrote excitedly to Schinkel from Manchester:

It is only here, my friend, that the machinery and buildings can be found commensurate with the miracles of modern times – they are

Cyfartha ironworks, Merthyr Tydfil, South Wales, in 1825. The painter Penry Williams shows the process by night, adding an almost infernal dimension to the scene and illuminating the splendid iron-roof structure to best effect.

called factories. Such a barn of a place is eight or nine storeys high, up to forty windows long and usually four windows deep . . . A mass of such buildings stand in very high positions dominating the surrounding area: in addition a forest of even higher steam-engine chimneys, so like needles that one cannot comprehend how they stay up, present a wonderful sight from a distance, especially at night when the thousands of windows are brightly illuminated with gas light.[9]

Schinkel knew that examination of the pioneering mills and factories would be informative, possibly offering new architectural forms as well as providing answers to many technological questions. En route to England he and Beuth had visited Charenton, outside Paris, and found the enterprise in the hands of a Birmingham iron-founder, Aaron Manby. The massive factory for steam engines, iron casting and rolling had been built by 500 Englishmen. On their way home, Schinkel and Beuth visited a factory in the Low Countries, at Verviers, which had been set up by another Englishman, William Cockerill, in 1799, since when the family had expanded their textile enterprises into Prussia, at Beuth's invitation.[10] At one stage the Cockerills were running more than 60 mills and factories across northern Europe.

In England, Schinkel's and Beuth's journey was not without its problems. At the Strutts' mills at Belper in Derbyshire they were refused entry, no doubt because they were suspected of being industrial spies, which to some extent they were. Yet Schinkel was generous enough to think the mills, even seen solely from the exterior, 'the most beautiful in England'. At Dudley, in the west Midlands, the pair were more fortunate. They were guided around the Gospel Oaks Ironworks where Schinkel recorded that no less than fifteen steam engines, several furnaces, rolling mills, tin-plating machines and drills were housed under an iron and tiled roof, its hollow iron columns ingeniously serving as rainwater down-pipes as well as structural support. Schinkel sketched details of the machinery and roof vaulting. Typically, the buildings were more ingenious than architecturally distinguished, more utilitarian than functional in any modern sense. At the neighbouring Wednesbury Oaks Iron Works, a more impressive and organized site, he carefully drew the 'fine new well laid-out plant' in his journal.

In Sheffield and Birmingham, as elsewhere, Schinkel was greatly struck by the forests of towering chimneys, 'tall obelisks' as he termed them, and in the Potteries of Staffordshire he found an archaic, Romantic strangeness in the cone-shaped bottle kilns and factories, giving 'wonderfully Egyptian-oriental forms' to the landscape.[11] Travelling north to Leeds, he admired Fenton Murray's circular engineering works, as well as John Marshall's famous flax mill (a predecessor of the Egyptian Temple Mills). In Glasgow, the observant Prussians noticed that the noxious steam from Tennants' chemical bleach works was carefully drawn off via underground pipes, before being discharged high into the atmosphere through massive chimneys.

Schinkel missed nothing, observing every detail – especially the unusual – and the succinct lines of his written journal are interspersed with swift sketches showing the construction of roofs, vaults, iron columns or steam-driven machinery. He was captivated by such a novel, opportunistic approach to construction, developing almost before his eyes. Although Schinkel was daily engaged in recording the technology of engineering and structural details, his broader architectural imagination also responded to the new forms of building that appeared at every turn.

Beuth proved an expert and knowledgeable guide. The pair visited the London machine shops of prolific engineer-inventors such as Joseph Bramah and Henry Maudslay, responsible for a gamut of patents, and perhaps, respectively, best known for the water closet and the screw-cutting lathe. In such workshops, a glance at the very roof overhead might reveal an iron part that had been adapted from its original purpose to serve some quite other structural use. Technology transfer was more often an accidental business than the result of forethought.

In Manchester, already acknowledged to be the world capital of the Industrial Revolution, Schinkel found extremes, of splendour and of horror. He recorded with admiration the skilled engineering of the canals, driven over and under the city, and the massive dimensions of the largest mills that now, confident of being virtually indestructible by fire, could afford to rise to seven or eight storeys and to exceed, he noted, even the length of the royal palace in Berlin. Schinkel learned that 400 factories had been built in Lancashire over the last ten years, yet many were already so smoke-blackened that they might have stood for 100 years. However well prepared he might have been by Beuth's reports, or by his own observations in the smoke-laden atmosphere of the Midlands and south Yorkshire, Schinkel was still utterly horrified by the scale and quality of the wider industrial landscape in Manchester: 'monstrous shapeless buildings put up only by foremen without architecture, only the least that was necessary and out of red brick'.

Schinkel took back to Prussia a repertory of forms, materials and sense of scale that would radically affect his own architectural design: few architects have been more profoundly influenced by industrial architecture. Ironically enough, he never designed a factory himself but the forms and materials of northern Britain crept into his work. Later, his pupil Heinrich Strack worked with August Borsig to develop heavy engineering works at Berlin-Moabit, a vast plant producing railway locomotives and iron structural components for other industrial buildings. The factory, designed as a showpiece in the Romanesque Revival style around a courtyard and entered through an impressive Classical screen, provides an insight as to how Schinkel might have approached such a commission.[12]

In Britain, as the mills proliferated and the harshness of labouring life became obvious, the image and reality of the factory became an increasingly dark one. Admiration for the new technology and the commercial success that it brought was tempered by periodic trade crises and a growing realization of the physical and moral costs of unrestrained and ill-considered industrial and urban growth. By the early 1830s cotton textiles amounted to half the nation's total exports and a booming engineering industry had been spawned. Yet, within a few months, a trade war over the high price of American cotton put paid to the expansion. Mills closed with terrible consequences. By the time that Friedrich Engels was reporting to Germany from Manchester, by now known by its sobriquet of Cottonopolis, it was the 'Hungry Forties'. If the late 1790s and the 1820s had been bad times, these were far worse. Even the most enlightened factory owners (almost all Dissenters and many of them Unitarian) had become deeply disillusioned. The fearsome sublimity of the 300-horsepower steam engines was one thing, the noxious fumes and heavy pall of smoke quite another. It fell to novelists such as Elizabeth Gaskell, Benjamin Disraeli and Charles Dickens to put the blackened image of the Northern factory on the page and take it into the drawing rooms of the South.

Elizabeth Gaskell, the wife of a Unitarian minister in Manchester, set her first novel, *Mary Barton*, against this background. A central episode is the devastating fire at Carson's mill, which is greeted almost as a blessing by the owners, happy to claim the insurance and rebuild their old factory and install the latest in modern machinery. That their factory hands are left with no work and no means of support is of little concern to the Carsons, comfortably housed nearby. No wonder that most leaders of Manchester's manufacturing society were aggrieved to discover the real identity of the author of *Mary Barton* on its publication in 1848.

North and South followed in 1854–5, initially serialized by Dickens in *Household Words*. Here Mrs Gaskell provides a more sympathetic mill owner, the foil to her heroine Margaret Hale, who has been uprooted from a vicarage shaded by ancient oaks in the New Forest to the grimly purposeful Milton-Northern. She leaves southern manners and certainties for a brusque world of brick, smoke and chance, as the companion of her father who has left the church to become a tutor. Even Mrs Gaskell's proud mill owner, Mr Thornton, with his 'dazzling . . . energy which conquered immense difficulties with ease' and his good conscience, which had caused him to adapt his factory chimneys so that they produced less poisonous smoke, falls foul of the times, losing the loyalty of his workforce and, nearly, his mill. At the opposite social and economic extreme is Margaret's friend, a 19-year-old factory girl dying of byssinosis, an asthmatic condition caused by breathing in cotton fluff, endemic in those mills without extraction fans in the carding sheds. Elizabeth Gaskell's pages are peppered with such facts; she was determined that her readers should not escape the truth.

The smoke that smudged in the horizon of many a topographic watercolour no longer appeared as a charmingly picturesque veil but as an insidious menace. Coketown, Charles Dickens's own Milton-Northern in *Hard Times* (possibly based upon Preston in Lancashire, which he had visited to report on striking workers in 1854), was a world of grey muslin curtains and smut-coated garden plants. Coal smoke encrusted the hard red brick and gold-grey stone of the mills and houses, blurring their features and colours, and it clogged the lungs, often to fatal effect. Later in his life, John Ruskin saw black clouds, with hallucinatory horror, billowing

THE SAME TOWN IN 1840

1. S! Michael's Tower rebuilt in 1750. 2. New Parsonage House & Pleasure Grounds. 3. The New Jail. 4. Gas Works. 5. Lunatic Asylum. 6. Iron Works & Ruins of S! Maries Abbey. 7. J! Evans Chapel. 8. Baptist Chapel. 9. Unitarian Chapel. 10. New Church. 11. New Town Hall & Concert Room. 12. Wesleyan Centenary Chapel. 13. New Christian Society. 14. Quakers Meeting. 15. Socialist Hall of Science.

Catholic town in 1440.

1. S! Michaels on the Hill. 2. Queens Cross. 3. S! Thomas's Chapel. 4. S! Maries Abbey. 5. All Saints. 6. S! Johns. 7. S! Peters. 8. S! Alkmunds. 9. S! Maries. 10. S! Edmunds. 11. Grey Friars. 12. S! Cuthberts. 13. Guild hall. 14. Trinity. 15. S! Olaves. 16. S! Botolphs.

across Lake Coniston (which they could never in reality reach), but even to a mind more clear and rational than his, smoke pollution had become unacceptable.[13] For his part, Ruskin had long since ceased to believe in benevolent manufacturers.

'Catholic town in 1440' and 'The same town in 1840', from A.W.N. Pugin, *Contrasts, or a Parallel between the Noble Edifices of the Middle Ages, and Similar Buildings of the Present Day; Shewing the Present Decay of Taste* (London, 2nd edn 1841). Pugin idealizes the pre-industrial era by a vivid 'before and after'.

Yet, despite the menacing image of the factory – epitomized in Augustus Welby Pugin's *Contrasts* (1836), in which the industrial landscape was compared to that of an idyllic, pre-industrial medieval past – and the forceful arguments about the dignity of labour that Ruskin and William Morris would use as the guiding principles of the Arts and Crafts movement, well-founded pride in technological progress and achievement could also provide a positive counterbalance.

Mrs Gaskell was a friend of both William Fairbairn and James Nasmyth, the leading engineers in Manchester, and, characteristically, did not feel that her sex precluded her from an intelligent interest in heavy engineering. In 1864 her friends provided an itinerary for one of her visitors. Among their suggestions for the 'things best worth seeing', in her words, was a spinning mill with the '*latest* improvements'; Whitworth's machinery works, 'if you do not get a stupid *fine* young man to show you over – try rather

Carl Eduard Biermann's heroic and optimistic painting of 1848 showing the new-built Borsig heavy engineering plant. The architectural aspirations of its architect, Heinrich Strack, a pupil of Schinkel, were soon forgotten as this part of Berlin became the city's industrial heart.

The Daily Express machine room, Fleet Street, London, designed by Owen Williams and published by the *Architectural Review* in 1932 – a stirring image of mechanization and functional form.

for one of the *working* men'; and another engineering works, Locketts, which had '*Very* clever *small* machinery'.[14]

Fifty years later, the resonances of the machine had changed beyond recognition. Abstracted mechanical imagery became a powerful strand in the arts in the early twentieth century, and the excitement of what came to be called the Machine Age was forcefully conveyed, sometimes doubling as an apt metaphor for political and social comment. A generation of photographers, film makers and artists, including Paul Strand, Charles Sheeler, Eisenstein and Fernand Léger, borrowed their subject matter from the landscape and technology of the manufacturing process and invested it with a new and intense visual presence. The sirens, whistles and klaxons that governed the coming and goings of the workforce and the routines they circumscribed continued to be the stuff of the best post-war social realist films – *Saturday Night and Sunday Morning* or the *Bicycle Thieves*. Otherwise, factory life and industrial activity went on somewhere well out of sight of most people's lives.

When the British war correspondent Alexander Werth arrived at his destination, Stalingrad, on a night of excruciating cold in February 1943, the Battle of Stalingrad had just ended, with the surrender of the German Sixth Army, a toll of deaths and injuries that ran to several millions and the obliteration of Stalin's model city. The only thing that he would see on the horizon at first light was, a Russian soldier told him, the Tractor Plant. 'It looks as if it were standing, but it's all gone.'

The next morning, Werth and his colleagues crawled out of the dugout, to find themselves in the remnants of a garden suburb. Far away, in the direction of the frozen Volga, 'one had the impression that there was . . . a live industrial town, but under

the chimneys were only the ruins of the Tractor Plant. Chimneys are among the hardest things to hit, and these were standing, seemingly untouched.'

When the party of journalists reached the spot, the fresh snow had been scraped off by a vicious wind. They found an unrecognizable terrain, pitted by bomb craters and riven by trenches. The only, ghastly, note of colour came from the frozen corpses, both Germans and Russians.

There was barbed wire here, and half-uncovered mines, and shell cases, and more rubble, and fragments of walls, and tortuous tangles of rusty steel girders but strange to say, though riddled with

A still from *Saturday Night and Sunday Morning*, in which repetitive working life in a Nottingham factory formed the background to Karel Reisz's powerful film of 1960.

holes, a large red-brick factory chimney was still standing, rising from all this . . . But now everything was silent and dead in this cold fossilised hell, as though a raving lunatic had suddenly died of heart failure.[15]

Little more than ten years earlier, this had been Henry Ford's model plant, designed by Albert Kahn Inc. of Detroit to produce the Fordson tractor, the engine of the promised Soviet agricultural

Anti-romanticism, conveyed by the towering chimneys of the Loewe engineering works in Berlin. Gustav Wunderwald's dark painting of 1929 was a strong contrast to the contemporary avant-garde celebration of every aspect of industrial imagery.

miracle. The very epitome of the Machine Age, a marriage of convenience had been contracted between the two opposing power blocks of the modern world. The wedding gift was an immense run of buildings more than a kilometre long, with glazed walls and a conveyor belt running its length, and even the latter – epitomizing moving assembly-line production and scientific management – was, fortunately, 'no longer an issue of disagreement between capitalists and socialists'. Latterly the tractors had given way to T-34 tanks. As late as September 1942, the factory carried on: 150 armoured cars and 200 tanks rolled off the assembly line as the Germans fought their way east.

The total destruction of the greatest of all the capitalist-communist showpiece factories in a last-ditch effort by the Axis powers as they fought their losing battle against Stalin's troops is one of the strangest ironies of modern times. The image of the factory was conclusively trampled into the filthy mud of the battlefield: there could be no more romanticism about industry.

2 Factory as Model: Early Versions

Architecture is always a set of actual monuments,
not a vague corpus of theory.
H. R. Hitchcock and Philip Johnson

The physical and social provisions of the early factory and its workforce were all too often rough and ready, the poor conditions in late eighteenth and early nineteenth-century mills and workplaces being mirrored by atrocious housing and negligible amenities. Such crude arrangements ignored the higher standards set in the first model industrial enterprises, while its own brutal excesses would point to new patterns for the future.

In Britain the first enlightened industrialists, engineers, entrepreneurs and inventors, such as Richard Arkwright, the Strutts and the Wedgwoods, set the pace, but in mainland Europe factory communities were the province of the ruling autocrat. Thus in architectural form, as in economic and social respects, they had much in common with the predetermined, hierarchical organization of the landed estate. Emphasizing the point, many of the first generation of manufactories in the Low Countries were housed in the castles, churches and monasteries that had been seized or expropriated during the French Revolution or under Austrian rule. The enclosed microcosm of factory and labour force soon attracted the attention of social and political theorists; for here was a society in miniature upon which larger, improved worlds could be founded. Architecture and plan provided an image and a structure, within which intriguing and important adjustments might be made.

Unsurprisingly enough, the plan chosen in 1781 for Louis XVI's royal iron-foundry, at Le Creusot in Burgundy, was that of a late seventeenth-century nobleman's estate. The realities and essentials of heavy industry, foundries, smelting sheds, furnaces and waste were resolutely shoehorned into a demesne in a curious simulacrum of the established order.

A substantial house for the Director, a 'proto-château', set in gardens and among *allées* of trees, lay at the apex of the horse-shoe plan, at the furthest point from the heat, noise and smoke of the foundry and workshops.[1] The blocks that would have traditionally accommodated the farm and domestic servants were transformed into living quarters for the workers, surrounded by vegetable gardens for their own use. Thus the grander *avant-cour* was, just as in the usual château plan, succeeded by a more utilitarian *basse-cour*. Enclosed within an ordered system, overseen by the Director in the big house, the long working hours of each day were resolutely measured out by a large clock, a prominent feature over the entrance to the main foundry block.

At Le Creusot, the heavy responsibility for transforming iron production by coke-smelting fell to William Wilkinson, one of a family of English ironmasters from Broseley, near Coalbrookdale, who had been invited to France initially to advise at another royal foundry near Nantes. When Arthur Young visited the works at Le Creusot in the tense weeks of August 1789 he reported the gossip: since Wilkinson was Joseph Priestley's brother-in-law 'and therefore a friend of mankind . . . he taught them to bore cannon, in order to give liberty to America'.[2] New technology has always tended to give rise to lively suspicion, if not fully formed conspiracy theories.

Wilkinson's worries were not, however, primarily political but practical, since there were great difficulties in applying the new

English system of coke smelting and puddling successfully in France. Nevertheless, the introduction of solid casting and boring along with steam power – Young counted five steam engines and another under construction – had given rise to a sizeable plant, designed and supervised by Pierre Toufaire, the leading French naval architect–engineer from Rochefort, whose experience of the scale and labour organization in the royal shipyard well equipped him to translate efficient working practices and living conditions into a plan that combined innovation and tradition.

Nearby, looking down from a small hill, was the Cristallerie de la Reine, built in 1786 in the form of a collegiate quadrangle, with the attics used for the workers' dormitories and the kilns, like vast table ornaments, placed on two outer corners.[3] The Cristallerie was an important planet in the orbit of the Le Creusot ironworks, as the queen was to the king.

The network of industries under royal protection, provided through subsidies, legal adjustments and tax breaks, had been modernized by Louis XIV's minister Colbert into a two-tiered system: the *Manufactures Royales* were encouraged by a range of

Print showing the Cristallerie de la Reine, Le Creusot, Burgundy, of 1786, its courtyard layout borrowed from châteaux of the period and siting the kilns at the extremities. Architect Barthélémy Jeanson.

preferential arrangements, while above them the *Manufactures d'Etat* – which included the Gobelins (according to Arthur Young 'such an one as could be supported only by a crowned head'), Sèvres and Saint-Gobain factories – benefited from the direct patronage of the king and court.

Across Europe, east from Prussia into Poland and Russia, south around the Mediterranean, the absolute rulers led a hectic programme of manufacturing expansion. The emphasis on luxury items – tapestries, porcelain, crystal and silk – is a reminder that the production of these factories was destined for a privileged inner circle, to clothe themselves and furnish their palaces, villas and residences in appropriate style. Much of the workforce consisted of highly skilled craftsmen. Near his summer palace at Caserta, the

Triumphant gateway into the royal silkworks built by the King of Naples in the 1780s. San Leucio, Caserta.

Ornamental detail alluding to the activities within. Former royal tobacco factory (now university), Seville, 1766, architect Sebastian van der Vorcht.

King of Naples rewarded his silk workers with well-built housing alongside the elegant Baroque factories of San Leucio. In Seville, the royal tobacco monopoly was housed in a factory complex that was second only to the Escorial in size and complexity. In all these industries, profits were either garnered directly by the royal sponsors or were raised through licensing, hence 'royalties'.

Other factories were also founded by royal or imperial edict to produce and process the raw materials and necessities for the state, whether in peace or wartime, essentials such as paper currency and coins, heavy engineering, ship building, plate glass and munitions among them. These factories reflected a rigid social and political reality, but also pointed the way to what might follow, as traditional, craft-based skills gave way, very unevenly, to new machinery, systems and organization of labour. The built form could act as an element of control, potentially replicable, within the overall bureaucracy.

So efficient and successful were some of these enterprises that they endured long beyond the dynasties of their founders; Napoleon III and Empress Eugénie were pictured visiting Louis XIV's Saint-Gobain plate-glass factory almost 200 years after its foundation, and the name lives on as a world-leading glass manufacturer. Equally, after the Revolution, Le Creusot would regain its position as France's leading ironworks – first under the brief ownership of another generation of English iron masters, Aaron Manby and David Wilson (who, as usual, imported an English workforce), and then, in a spectacular expansion, under the ownership of the Schneider family.

In architectural terms, the boldest project of all was Claude-Nicolas Ledoux's royal saltworks in eastern France at Arc-et-Senans, near Besançon. During his later chequered professional career, Ledoux would toy with innumerable exercises in pure geometry, absolute symmetry and architectural reason, never to be realized, but his youthful project, the building of the Saline de Chaux, would allow him to claim with justification that he had joined 'the interests of art with those of government'.[4]

Heavily salinated springs under the eastern range of the Jura mountains had long provided a valuable source of salt, from which could be extracted the recently imposed and highly lucrative salt tax, the *gabelle*, which with the tobacco tax was a major source of royal revenue and as such a loathed imposition on all but the exempted aristocracy. The powerful tax collectors, the Farmers-General, wanted to found a Royal Factory closer to the forest of Chaux, from which they could obtain virtually limitless fuel. At the same time the process, little changed for many centuries, needed modernization. Ledoux's ideas ranged further still; in Anthony Vidler's words, he was determined to design 'a far-from-commonplace factory, one that from the outset he conceived as taking its place as a productive centre, a rapidly expanding "natural city" in the fertile but barely exploited territory of the Jura and Franche-Comté'.

Ledoux, in post as a Commissioner for the saltworks of the region from 1771, was from his own observations well aware of the need for urgent improvements both to product and process. He drew up a first project for an immense, but conventional, rectilinear scheme for a saltworks and workers' village, finalized well before the death of Louis XV in early 1774. A few months later he altered tack and submitted a completely new semicircular version, the Classical model for which was the perfection of the plan of the archetypal Roman theatre as described by Vitruvius in *De Architectura.*

In early 1775 the foundation stone was laid and four years later the job was finished. On a purely aesthetic level, Ledoux would

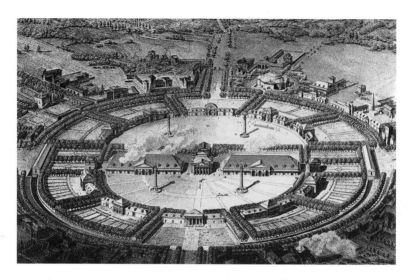

describe the idealized scheme (which he later expanded, on paper, into an ellipse) as being 'as pure as the trajectory described by the sun', but he also claimed a practical justification for the rearrangement from quadrangle to semicircle, considering that it separated the various noxious and inflammable operations of the Saline more effectively from the workers' housing.

Ledoux's neo-Classical scheme, detailed in a heavy Mannerist fashion, consists of an open crescent of ten major buildings, built of stone and brick, of varying heights and dimensions, roof lines and fenestration. At the hub sits the Director's house, almost dwarfed by the imposing scale and nature of its dependencies. Entry is through the imposing gatehouse, a propylaeum that was ornamented as a grotto, the stone tortuously carved into encrustation, as if water is solidifying into salt before your eyes. Elsewhere the architectural orders and heavy rustication are used to limited but impressive effect; early visitors were surprised to find such grandeur ('columns in a factory!', exclaimed one).

Perspective View of the Town of Chaux, Claude-Nicolas Ledoux's planned community in the Franche-Comté of 1804, which he envisaged as an expanded version of the royal saltworks, completed many years earlier.

Heavily rusticated columns mark the entrance to the Director's house at the Saline de Chaux, with a wing of the saltworks beyond. 1775–8, architect Claude-Nicolas Ledoux.

The Director's 'house' formed the keystone to the arc of Ledoux's ground plan. It was the control point of the works, housing the administration and the supervisors, who were lodged in attics behind the pediment. Ledoux called it the 'temple de surveillance'. On the general plan, the sight lines from the Director's house to the rest of the complex were marked in. Every vestige of authority at the Saline de Chaux emanated from here, including the spiritual, for there was a chapel, and the temporal, in the form of a courtroom.

Each of the workers' pavilions in the crescent had a double-height core around a central chimney, with dormitories for the workers to either side. Evaporation of the brine, over great charcoal-fired furnaces, took place in two low, heavily roofed wings. The plan reflected the rigid ordering of men, materials, time and end product.

The main entrance to the Saline, through a triumphal gateway and grotto.
The Director's house can be seen in the distance.

The royal saltworks was never to reach its hoped-for output level, faulty wooden pipes being a major problem from the beginning of production, in October 1778. Its fate became uncertain during the Revolution and following the abolition of the loathed salt tax. At one point, conversion to another use, such as textile printing, was considered, but in 1795 an official report found good organization and efficiency at the works. Commercial production continued until the 1890s.

At the Saline de Chaux the rigorous requirements of the royal manufacture were subsumed within a living architectural model of perfect order, control and schematic design. After the Revolution and his fall from favour, Ledoux amused himself by elaborating the plan into an extended ideal town, simply by completing the circle and adding outlying buildings beyond. Around the periphery of Chaux would be a ring of heavy industry, ironworks, glass kilns,

The saltworks, ornamented by stone water-spouts that graphically express the process, appearing to solidify into salt.

porcelain factories and textile mills. The engraving of the cannon factory with its belching kilns owes much to models such as the Cristallerie at Le Creusot and the earlier widely admired Wedgwood works at Etruria. 'The cross axis of the Saline joins the routes to Arc and Senans, the forges of Roche, the paper mills, the polishing mills; what activity! Some polish the steel, chase the brass, blow the crystal, others cast the molten metal that sustains the rights of nations.'[5] By temperament Ledoux was a believer in considered institutional change, and his published scheme represented his ideas of the reordering of economic power rather than of political revolution.

At its heart, the diagrammatic scheme for Chaux was driven by the notion of social order and economic efficiency. As at Le Creusot, the Director's house was all-seeing at the hub of the working wheel, a dynamic (if largely symbolic) inducement to time-keeping, productivity and moral rectitude.

The notion of a rational form of organization for industry was tempting. If working practices and processes were properly under-

The rational approach to industry. Claude-Nicolas Ledoux's schematic plan for a proposed cannon foundry for the town of Chaux, published in 1804.

stood, it was necessary, wrote Ledoux with an apparent early grasp of scientific management, 'to conform to the needs and conveniences of a productive factory where the utilization of time offers a first economy'. Both ground plans and architectural forms might be excellent signals of intent.

Much has been made, by Michel Foucault and others, of the importance of surveillance in the design of late eighteenth-century institutions. To enforce efficiency in an unskilled, possibly casual, workforce was no mean task, and a logical geometry evolved to ensure a high quality, mass-produced commodity. The physical and moral well-being of the workforce was essential to the process, translated at the saltworks at Chaux into workers' accommodation and vegetable gardens. In reality, the 200 workers found themselves in a highly circumscribed society, cut off from the outside world by a massive wall topped with thorn branches and a dry moat, behind a forbidding entrance lodge, the gates of which were rarely open and were attended by liveried guards, initially wearing the uniform of the king.

At much the same time, in Russia, Catherine the Great's favourite, Prince Potemkin, was developing ambitious plans to turn the Krichev estate – annexed from Poland in 1772 and granted to him by the empress in 1776 – into a major industrial centre, river port and trading area. The empress was keen to promote Russian manufacturing industry by granting serfs to important enterprises, such as Sir Charles Baird's iron and sugar works in St Petersburg, and, in so doing, building up a skilled workforce.[6]

In 1784 Potemkin handed over responsibility for Krichev to a young English engineer named Samuel Bentham. On arrival he found the site in an extremely poor state, but within two years he had made such progress in modernizing and organizing the mills, distilleries and factories that he offered personally to take over the running of the least successful ventures for a ten-year period, asking Potemkin only for a £5,000 loan, to be repaid over the years.[7]

The problem that Bentham faced was the management of a large polyglot and unskilled serf labour force. The difficulties of organizing them, making them answerable to discipline and supervision while reaching even minimal levels of output, were daunting. The problem quickly sparked a solution in Bentham's mind that took a physical form. If supervision could be established in the centre of a common space, from a higher vantage point, then the task became feasible. From there, a single individual might oversee large numbers of workers. At the same time, Jeremy Bentham, Samuel's brother, had been involved in recruiting labour for the enterprise in England and became increasingly eager to join his brother in Russia. Even from a distance, Jeremy Bentham saw Russia as the ideal test-bed for his own theories of social organization. The degraded serf was a more malleable creature than an independent Englishman, however impoverished. In early 1786 Bentham arrived in Krichev.[8]

Once there, Jeremy Bentham did little to help his brother, burying himself in his theoretical work, developing the theory of 'central observation', which would, he believed, be applicable to a range of building types, schools, prisons and hospitals as well as factories. With the help of Samuel's engineering knowledge and skills as a draughtsman, together with the practical and structural experience of an English master bricklayer, the plans were worked up in detail. The Ukraine might well have seen the prototype industrial Panopticon (literally, an all-seeing eye), had it not been for Potemkin's impulsive sale of the entire estate in 1787.

In the event the developed structure, presented as a model penitentiary with possibilities as a workhouse, factory or even poultry

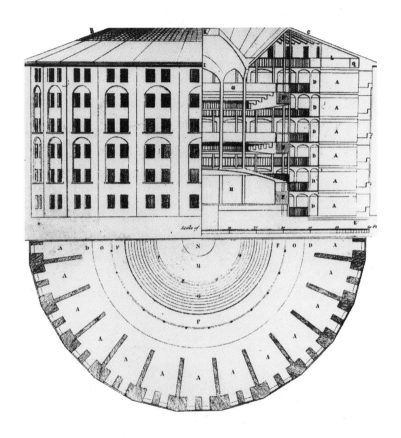

house, was offered to a far wider public through the pages of Bentham's published account – *Panopticon, or The Inspection House* (1791) – after his return to London. He pointed out that while those who worked on a piecework system needed no coercion, those working on fixed hours required overseeing. The new building type, he claimed, would send a current of clean air through society. 'Morals reformed – health preserved – industry

Jeremy Bentham's design, made in 1791, for the multi-purpose Panopticon.

invigorated – instruction diffused . . . all by a simple idea in Architecture!'

Brigadier-General Sir Samuel Bentham, who in later life became Inspector-General of Naval Works, held fast to the idea; in 1807 a Panopticon was built at Ochta, near St Petersburg, as a training centre for naval manufactures; and back home in 1812 he unsuccessfully tried to persuade the Admiralty to plan a new naval arsenal at Sheerness in Kent on the lines of the Panopticon. As a factory, an inflexible, centrally planned building proved wholly unsuitable for changing manufacturing processes and machinery. For all the hopes and rhetoric vested in the form, the Panopticon never proved itself to be a replicable physical model for industry, although it fared rather better as a prison.[9]

A far more promising way to reorganize society was to take an existing factory or mill along with its workers and transform the conditions of their work and lives. A physically enclosed world offered intriguing possibilities for different versions of organizational reform, an ideal structural and political canvas for social experiment. When Robert Owen moved from the cotton mills of

The 'round building', or Panopticon, Belper, Derbyshire, built by the pioneering Strutts in 1811–13. This variant of the form was a rare industrial version, which quickly proved inflexible and impractical. It was demolished in 1959.

Manchester and became David Dale's son-in-law and business partner in New Lanark (in which the ubiquitous Richard Arkwright had been briefly involved), he immediately saw the potential for a reorganization that went far beyond matters of daily working practice, although his own intellectual journey towards a socialism that freed men from concerns of property or profit would take much longer.

The New Lanark Twist Company was sited in a valley in Strathclyde next to a spectacular waterfall and consisted of four cotton mills, a number of workshops and some tenement housing. From the time of his arrival in 1799, Owen began to apply his progressive ideas about factory management: the cooperation he gained by showing respect for his workers and managers ensured a high quality product and, hence, a profitable enterprise, which enabled him to finance his idealistic ventures.[10] That these, in turn, were rooted in such a patently orderly and successful venture helped to give credibility to his model community.

In 1812 Owen dissolved his former partnership and quickly brought in new partners, fellow idealists, the Quaker William

The clean and orderly premises at the Shaker Center Family Medicine Factory, Mount Lebanon, New York, photographed in 1931, where the Shakers prepared herbs for distribution and sale.

Allen, who later set up his own Sussex land settlement, and Jeremy Bentham. The timing was unfortunate, since the wars with America had lowered cotton prices dramatically, but Owen was not deterred from his notion that the rural mill town offered a perfect test-bed for his theories of 'social psychology and economic philosophy'.[11] He envisaged that New Lanark, then merely one of many water-powered textile mills in the countryside beyond Glasgow, would eventually stand apart, the working exemplar of his utopian 'New System of Society', as laid out in his *A New View of Society* (1813).

Owen's views on the iniquities of the Factory System, in particular on the use of child labour, guided the way in which he ran New Lanark, a canny mixture of the carrot and the stick. He quickly outlawed the employment of pauper children and insisted that education be the central plank within his raft of ideas. The Institute for the Formation of Character (the lofty name he had chosen for his school) opened on New Year's Day in 1816, and was

The late 18th-century main block of the mills at New Lanark, South Lanarkshire, Scotland, the site for Robert Owen's brave experiment.

organized to follow the educational reformer Johann Heinrich Pestalozzi's guiding principles of kindness and common sense. Children were offered full-time education until the age of 10, before beginning work in the mills, but were encouraged to continue their schooling with evening classes thereafter. For their parents' benefit, he reduced working hours while closely evaluating output with the use of a 'silent monitor', recording each worker's efforts according to a system of colour markers. There were curfews and fines for drunkenness, yet during the American embargo on cotton exports he continued to pay his workforce and instituted a sick fund and communal kitchens and dining rooms.

Owen's dealings with government, which included giving evidence on the Poor Laws and the proposed Factory Acts based on his own wide experience, radicalized him further. In 1817 he published a letter to London newspapers in which he contrasted life in manufacturing towns against his proposed Villages of Co-operation, a scheme drawn up to counter 'the depreciation of human labour . . . occasioned by the general introduction of mechanism into the manufactures of Europe and America, but principally into those of Britain, where the change was greatly accelerated by the inventions of Arkwright and Watt'.[12] In his villages mechanization would be limited and the factory balanced with the farm.

Sir Robert Peel's Factory Act, which was passed in 1819, introduced the notion of government intervention in private industry and was followed, at lengthy intervals, by further measures. The Act, becoming law under a Tory prime minister who was himself a mill owner's son, had been weakened from the original, wide-ranging draft for which Robert Owen had fought so tenaciously. As passed, it applied only to children working in cotton mills (acknowledged to be the toughest sector of the textile industry), outlawed the employment of children under 9 years of age and

THE CRISIS,

OR THE CHANGE FROM ERROR AND MISERY, TO TRUTH AND HAPPINESS

1832.

IF WE CANNOT YET

LET US ENDEAVOUR

RECONCILE ALL OPINIONS,

TO UNITE ALL HEARTS.

IT IS OF ALL TRUTHS THE MOST IMPORTANT, THAT THE CHARACTER OF MAN IS FORMED FOR — NOT BY HIMSELF.

Design of a Community of 2,000 Persons, founded upon a principle, commended by Plato, Lord Bacon, Sir T. More, & R. Owen.

EDITED BY
ROBERT OWEN AND ROBERT DALE OWEN.

London:
PRINTED AND PUBLISHED BY J. EAMONSON, 15, CHICHESTER PLACE,
GRAY'S INN ROAD.
STRANGE, PATERNOSTER ROW: PURKISS, OLD COMPTON STREET,
AND MAY BE HAD OF ALL BOOKSELLERS.
1833.

13. Title page of *The Crisis*

limited the hours worked by older children to no more than twelve hours in twenty-four. The operation of Owen's own system at New Lanark had been, in essence, his plea for a far more radical Factory Act. An authoritarian regime based upon temperance, economy and strict discipline, it also offered a humane version of employment standards in factories.

In that year of the first Factory Act, visitors flocked to New Lanark; one American observer was highly impressed by Owen's achievement, noticing that the mills closed at 6.30 p.m. so that workers could benefit from further education, music and dancing, the last in Owen's view a particularly relaxing and suitable diversion. The visitor reported that 'there is not . . . to be found in any part of the world, a manufacturing village . . . composed of persons indiscriminately brought together, without any peculiar bond of

The frontispiece to *The Crisis* (London, 1833), in which Owen adds his name to those of Plato, Bacon and More, and an architectural vision of Utopia.

fraternity, in which so much order, good government, tranquillity and rational happiness prevail'.[13] Robert Southey, the poet, thought the mills 'perfect of their kind, according to the present state of mechanical science', being clean, well ventilated and not unpleasant smelling. But when the schoolchildren were asked to perform for him he was uncomfortably reminded of a line of Dutch cows, their tails wagging in unison.[14]

The one element that disturbed even the most admiring of visitors – and which had contributed to the breakup of Owen's partnership with Allen and Bentham – was the complete lack of religious observance. Robert Owen's dismissal of religious-based communities, on principle, blinded him (or perhaps simply made him unwilling to admit) to the important lessons in social and spatial organization offered by both the Moravian and the Shaker communities. By giving formal expression to self-imposed individual regulatory limits, familial and sexual, as their collective aspirations – those of economic self-sufficiency based upon skilled trades and agriculture – they were models that could have served Owen well. The plan of Fairfield, the Moravian village outside Manchester, with its square within a square, drawn up by a very young Benjamin Henry Latrobe – long before he turned his attention to the public buildings of Washington, DC – and the subtle, mirror-image Shaker buildings in which the sexes never met, are superbly contrived, communally agreed, determinist devices.[15] Self sufficiency was a major objective for the Shakers, and the large community at Mount (New) Lebanon, in New York state, boasted industrial-scale premises by the early years of the nineteenth century. The men ('brothers') made brooms and packaged garden seeds as well as following heavier occupations, such as light engineering and milling. The women ('sisters') had their own substantial three-storey workshop where, among many other activities, they bottled and packed herbs and essences.

Over the years, Owen had travelled widely to present his ideas and blueprints for an improved society, visiting figures such as Napoleon on Elba, Tsar Alexander I and President John Quincy Adams. But New Lanark, and his voluminous writings, would prove to be the only enduring testament to his theories. In 1824 he left Scotland for America, aiming to revolutionize a wider world with multiplying Villages of Co-operation: in the event only the limping New Harmony in Indiana justified his journey west.

Robert Owen's ideas had initially fallen on very fertile ground, for the urgent dilemma in North America was how to retain an agrarian society that remained in step with the march of urbanization. In 1816 Thomas Jefferson had written: 'while we have land to labour . . . for the general operation of manufacture, let our workshops remain in Europe'.[16] Jefferson, who had set up a nail factory in the 1790s on his own plantation at Monticello, Virginia, envisaged a closed circle in which manufacture would supply the immediate needs of the Republic, avoiding the pitfalls of the industrial city and maintaining the agricultural economy. Humphreysville, Connecticut, illustrated the Jeffersonian idea of 'factories in the fields'; the eponymous founder, David Humphreys, had returned from his post as American minister to Spain and Portugal to set up a factory village around a textile mill from 1806. His workers were largely orphans and New England farmers' daughters, who were housed in lodging houses with gardens. They were carefully superintended, in all matters relating to 'education, manners, discipline, morals, and religion'.

Everything across the Atlantic was measured against the British experience. A vile picture of fouled landscapes and formless industrial cities, of degraded labour and negligible amenities was

quickly emerging. Francis Cabot Lowell visited Britain in 1810–11 and took particular interest in Manchester. On his return he set about inventing a power loom, found business partners (from his New England peer group) and a site on the Charles River at Waltham, Massachusetts, where the first mechanized cotton mill in America was built. The Boston Manufacturing Company, as the partnership was named, perfected what became known as the Lowell system, in which the corporation bought and developed a site and then leased the land off to individual companies. Lowell's venture was to prove immensely profitable for its promoters. By 1821 the company needed to expand and a new site was chosen, East Chelmsford on the Merrimack River, which benefited from a canalized system to provide water power.

Lowell had died in 1817, but his two business partners carried on, with a third associate, and gave their new city his name. By the end of 1823 the first mill was in production; in 1835 the railway came; and by 1848 Lowell had a population of 33,000. The careful pacing and diminutive scale of manufacturing industry in America had suddenly been exploded to massive proportions, but the fate of Lowell, with its Massachusetts sister towns Lawrence and Manchester, remained the litmus test of whether 'the

Terraced workers' boarding houses, Booth cotton mills, Lowell, Massachusetts, 1836.

Manufacturing system is compatible with the social virtues', as one observer wondered.

Watching Britain, struggling to contain the monster it had created, the Americans were taking stock. In New England there was a concerted policy to keep factories out of cities, and the American Society for the Encouragement of Domestic Manufactures pictured them 'on chosen sites, by the fall of waters and the running stream, the seats of health and cheerfulness, where good instruction will secure the morals of the young and good regulations will promote, in all, order, cleanliness, and the exercise of civil duties'.[17] Optimism remained the norm and few voices echoed Herman Melville when he wrote about his fear of the machine, 'this inflexible iron animal'.

With high hopes vested in it, Lowell became an object of intense curiosity – just like Coalbrookdale or New Lanark before it, or the Ford works in Detroit after it – but here with the emphasis strongly on the quality of working and living conditions. Could a starry-eyed American experiment marry capitalistic endeavour with moral idealism? Perceptive and well-informed visitors came, including Harriet Martineau and Charles Dickens, who were well placed to compare the American venture against the unhappy English experience.

A small guidebook was produced in 1848, advising 'the stranger' to obtain a note of introduction to the agent of each company in order to tour the various establishments, which numbered ten huge works and many smaller enterprises. The early mills had spawned printworks, carpet companies, bleach and dye works, as well as engineering and machine factories. By now many mills were rebuilding, expanding and converting to steam power. The Merrimack Manufacturing Company, oldest and largest of the companies, had recently built a mill 350 feet (106.68 m)

Cotton mills on the water, Hamilton Mills, Lowell, Massachusetts, 1840s, now a museum complex.

long powered by two turbine wheels and a new 'picker house' divided into two as a fire precaution. The completion of a top-lit carpet factory was celebrated with a picnic for 5,000, with music and '100 sets of cotillons' on the floor. 'Every one in this vast assemblage, clad with extreme neatness, and conducting themselves with good breeding and decorum, afforded by another proof of the superiority and refinement of the class of operatives in Lowell'. If the booklet was to be believed, Lowell was a model community – at play as at work.

When Charles Dickens paid his visit to Lowell in 1842 he was struck by the cleanliness of it all, both the people and the town, with its crisp red and white buildings, neat streets and trees. He noticed the factory windows carefully shaded from the sun by leafy green house plants, the salubrious boarding houses in which the largely female workforce was lodged and amenities such as the hospital and savings bank. Dickens realized that the workers had a long, hard day – twelve hours – and that there were a few children employed in the mills, but he still felt that there was no comparison to be made with conditions at home.

Some twenty years later, Anthony Trollope arrived, just as cotton supplies from the Southern states had been interrupted by the Civil War. Some mills were closed and short-time working had been introduced in many more. Even then he declared: 'It is Utopia'. But Utopia had its limitations; 'Lowell is a very wonderful place and shows what philanthropy can do; but I fear it also shows what philanthropy cannot do.' How, he mused, could Chicago with its population of 120,000 learn from this 'closed' system? Starting from scratch, the States have 'resolved . . . to avoid the evils' of industrialized England. Trollope was impressed that 'Good and thoughtful men have been active to spread education, to maintain health, to make work compatible with comfort and personal dignity', but concluded that when 'New England employs millions in her factories, instead of thousands . . . she must cease to provide for them their beds and meals, their church-going proprieties and orderly modes of life'.[18]

Titus Salt in England had more modest aims than the founders of Lowell but agreed with John Ruskin that it was the manufacturer's duty 'to make the various employments involved in the production, or transference of it, most beneficial to the men employed'. Salt had witnessed the unchecked development of the textile industry across the Pennines and wanted to break the mould. At the same time, he fully recognized that working families living in decent houses and benefiting from amenities that ranged from public baths to savings banks would also form a more stable workforce, to the great benefit of the productivity of the business. It was this realization, in which the paternalism of an enlightened industrialist met the pragmatism of the experienced manufacturer, that drove the progressive experiments in industrial settlements in Britain and elsewhere in the second half of the nineteenth century.

In 1851 Salt turned to the engineer and manufacturer William Fairbairn for expertise and experience, and together they planned and built a model industrial settlement around a vast mill, sited well away from Bradford in open countryside. Over it all towered the factory chimney, modelled on an Italian campanile. The housing in Saltaire carefully reflected the hierarchies of the workplace, with the ends of the terraces marked by larger houses for the foremen and a dignified terrace of almshouses for the elderly. There were places of worship, schools, a library and adult institute, all sited well upwind of the factory. Railway transport was provided so that the workers and their families could get to the nearby moors,

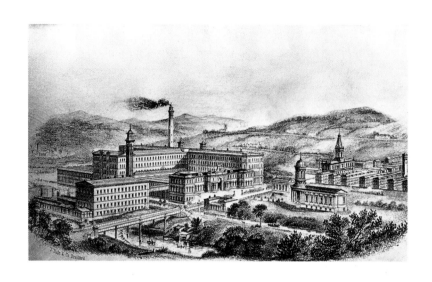

A contemporary print of Saltaire, near Bradford, West Yorkshire. The Italian-style alpaca mill towers over the model village, built from 1851 onwards by Titus Salt.

Saltaire. The mill and chimney designed by the engineer William Fairbairn are an impressive backdrop to the stone-built workers' housing, built on a neat grid.

but such paternalism had its downside too: washing lines were forbidden and people had to pay to use the communal laundry.

Gazing at the finished product, the editor of the *Birmingham Post* mused that this

> realisation of a great idea . . . has . . . shown what can be done towards breaking down the barrier which has existed between the sympathies of the labourer and the employer . . . No finer picture could be imagined by the dreamer . . . than that of a city where education is open to every child, – where labour is respected, – where intemperance is banished – where the graces of life and the higher intellectual pleasures are open to the enjoyment of all . . .[19]

Salt's enterprise was a model for the times, of interest as much abroad as at home.

Across Europe different variants upon the industrial settlement emerged. Jean-Baptiste Godin had become a follower of the utopian socialism of Charles Fourier in 1843 and continued to pursue his ideas while developing his iron-foundry and metalworks. In 1858 he began to build an industrial community around his domestic stove factory at Guise, in north-east France, calling it the *familistère.* He thus implied both links to Fourier's theoretical communal building, the *phalanstère*, and differences, in particular, his disagreement with Fourier's contempt for traditional family structures. At Guise, Godin built three linked residential blocks with internal balconies ranged around glass-roofed central courtyards, social spaces that would draw together the village-sized population. Thoughtful planning and high quality services (ventilation, running water and toilets on every floor) all helped to raise 'the moral and intellectual standards of the population',[20] which

Glazed internal court at communal workers' housing, seen in the mid-1970s. Built, following the ideas of the utopian Charles Fourier, for the Godin domestic stove factory at Guise, Picardy, c. 1858.

were underlined by profit-sharing and voting rights. By the early 1880s there were four blocks of housing and a wide range of amenities, including baths, nursery and primary school, dining hall, theatre and gymnasium.

Enlightened industrialists throughout Europe and North America organized their own piecemeal variants upon the model factory settlement and the social experiment. Each laid particular emphasis upon health and well being, sobriety and literacy. Housing was almost always tied to the job, just as on the landed estate, but the more progressive also allowed non-employees to rent their cottages. This was the case at Bournville near Birmingham, where Cadbury provided new housing with generous gardens, and at New Earswick outside York, built by Rowntree. Both chocolate-makers were Quakers – religious non-

The chocolate-makers Bournville called their works 'the factory in a garden', one of many efforts by enlightened industrialists to improve the face of late 19th-century working life.

conformity was the norm in the circles of nineteenth-century philanthropic industrialists.

At Bournville, the works carried the epithet 'the factory in a garden', and the workers could practice callisthenics on the lawns or while away their rest periods lounging by the ornamental ponds. Far away in the cigar-making city of Ybor in southern Florida, immigrant employees at one establishment had the benefit of a 'lector', who read selected stories from the daily trilingual newspaper from a central lectern as the Cuban workers below wrapped the cigars. In an era predating any state welfare provision, each company stood over its employees in a position of great power and responsibility.

Port Sunlight, as William Hesketh Lever, the future 1st Viscount Leverhulme, must have admitted to himself, was an absurd name to choose for the bleak tract of marshland that he bought in 1887, close to the Mersey estuary, some distance from Birkenhead. On moving from overcrowded, inadequate premises in Warrington, where the success of Lever's business had quickly forced him to extend the original factory building into a ramshackle collection of wooden sheds alongside, he dignified his intentions and his 20 hectares with the new name of his product. Sunlight soap was his choice, after recent legislation tightening up on trade descriptions had forced the energetic wholesale grocer to abandon the epithet 'pure honey' for his individually packed yellow soap bars.

The factory, as extensive as Warrington had been cramped, was the first building on the waterside site, with a wharf running alongside. While the design work was going on, Lever was continuously at the side of his architect, William Owen, ensuring that his personal contributions to the scheme were carried through. Eventually, his own office was to be perched high above the general administration block, its walls glazed so that he could keep a

An aerial view of Bournville, outside Birmingham, showing generous gardens and comfortable houses built in the late 1880s around the factory, for workers and others.

An aerial view of W. H. Lever's Port Sunlight, Merseyside. The soap factory is in the distance, the art gallery an unlikely focus for a model industrial village.

close eye on everything that occurred below. The workforce was well provided for, but never far from his sight.[21]

Nearby, Port Sunlight village was built in an eclectic mixture of English domestic styles and materials, its terraces ranged picturesquely over the large site. The houses were the antithesis of the industrial terraces of the North-West: colourful, architecturally varied, with modern conveniences and set in acres of grass and trees, the strongest possible contrast to the sooty back-to-backs of Birkenhead or Liverpool.

Yet after a long day at work, as Lever's (largely female) employees returned to their salubrious and well-appointed cottages, most of them half-timbered or tile-hung and seemingly taken from the pages of some book on the charms of Olde England, they still could not easily forget that the factory lay just beside the village. Its huge chimneys overshadowed their own and a pervasive smell of soap was carried everywhere on the breeze. Port Sunlight was there to make a wider point: its name, like its image, reinforcing a vision of apple-cheeked good housekeeping. There was no escaping the obligation towards domestic and personal propriety conveyed by the well-kept grounds and the public amenities, which included the Institute and Art Gallery but excluded a public house.

At Port Sunlight, as elsewhere, the housing was a variant on profit-sharing, in which the employees' dues were converted into low rents. The all-embracing paternalism of the firm and the dependency exacted from the workforce still chafed in the 1970s, long after Lever's death.[22] Unilever still operates at Port Sunlight, but under transformed conditions.

Port Sunlight was one of a pair with Lever's Thornton Hough, his estate village near the family mansion on the Wirral in Cheshire, and was designed by the same architects. There, in the countryside, the new cottages in their vocabulary of revivalist

styles looked on to the village green, with the church tower replacing the smokestacks of the works. Here, agricultural activities replaced industrial ones, but the imagery was much the same. Back at Port Sunlight, in the shadow of the works, the little garden suburb, with its beautifully tended open spaces and dignified public buildings, was a clear celebration of the domestic virtues and traditional values.

Lord Leverhulme's employees may have been unwitting participants in his empire of cleaning materials, but the village quickly became an international model for those considering how to realign industry, the countryside and the city at the end of the nineteenth century. This was the essential paradox with which the promoters of the late nineteenth-century model factory, the planners of the Garden Cities and New Towns, as well as men with such differing visions as Henry Ford and Tomás Bata, would wrestle in the early years of the next century.

Housing at Port Sunlight, Merseyside, seen shortly after its completion in the 1890s. The contrived allusion to traditional rural architecture served Lever well, serving both a moral and commercial purpose.

3 | Modern Models

I envy the architects of purposeful industrial buildings.
Frank Lloyd Wright

By the turn of the century, a new model was in place that sought to make industry a better neighbour than it had proved to be so far. Ebenezer Howard's idea of the Garden City began life as a polemic, the ideas culled from his familiarity with the USA, where he had gone in the early 1870s as a settler in rural Nebraska – quickly defeated by hand-to-mouth rural subsistence – before going to Chicago, where he became a shorthand writer. While there, he read widely and freely 'undisturbed by party feeling, class, religious or professional bias' while observing the explosion in property values in a city amidst the throes of post-fire rebuilding. Before he returned to London in 1876, intent on social reform as well as on his invention of an improved typewriter mechanism, he had already begun to gather ideas for 'an intelligently arranged town, a sort of marriage between town and country, whereby the workers would be assured the advantages of fresh air and recreation and nearness to their work.'[1]

The eventual outcome was a slim tract, published in 1898, entitled *Tomorrow: A Peaceful Path to Real Reform*. Howard revised and reissued it in 1902 as *Garden Cities of Tomorrow* with a number of diagrams that clarified his ideas of a central city (population 58,000) with a circle of roughly half-size satellite settlements.

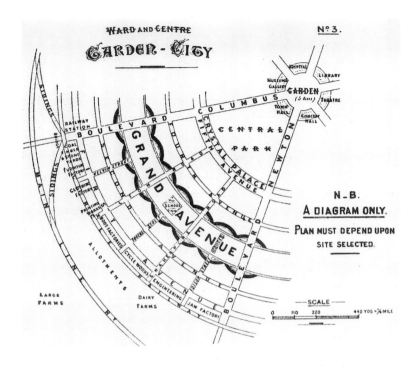

GARDEN - CITY

He could not imagine reforming the existing industrial chaos and so chose to make a fresh start. Despite his own naivety, his ideas appealed to an idealistic and interventionist generation and rapidly led to the establishment of the First Garden City, Letchworth in Hertfordshire, in which strict zoning, communal land holding and a full provision of amenities were central to its development. The new century was a moment for pipe dreams of novel urban forms, such as Tony Garnier's infinitely expandable iron-and-concrete zoned *Cité industrielle*, first exhibited in Paris in 1904 (but not published until 1917). The international acclaim that followed the modest conventionality and traditional allusions of the Garden City suggested that it was a workable model.

Ebenezer Howard's schematic plan for his projected garden city, with the industrial ring last but one. From *Garden Cities of Tomorrow* (1902).

Howard's work was translated into many languages, including Russian in 1904, and in 1913 the Russian Garden City Society was founded. In the vast spaces to the east of Europe, new patterns could be drawn on a clean sheet of paper, the open countryside.

In his publication, Howard suggested that the Garden City should be a wheel, with the railway station and the industrial quarter as the outer rim, intermediaries between the city and the countryside. The boot and jam factories, the works for the manufacture of bicycles, clothing and furniture, as well as those for printing and engineering, would neatly encircle the town, before it dissolved into the pleasant greenery of allotments and dairy farms. In Howard's clean subdivision of home, work and leisure, light industrial activity was the preamble to the countryside. In his pages, the problem of where to put the modern factory was solved.

Letchworth Garden City provided a practical test for the idea even if it did not follow Howard's perfect diagrammatic sequence of concentric circles. Barry Parker's and Raymond Unwin's plan of 1904 delineated a generous factory zone to the east of the site, near the railway and the recreation ground. Energetic efforts were made to attract businesses and the first lease was signed in 1905. Early arrivals were printing and specialist engineering works and the emphasis on skilled, light manufacture enabled the factories to affect an almost domestic image. When the Phoenix Car company relocated from north London in 1910, it conscientiously built a works that looked as little like a factory as possible, with a neat white-rendered office building as its public face. The vehicles were hand-crafted, made from metal sheeting nailed on to a wooden framework. Each radiator was ornamented by a phoenix.

For Spirella, an American corset company seeking a toehold in Europe, Letchworth, with its ample cottages, neatly hedged gardens,

integrated facilities and liberal credentials, was clearly a perfect setting for the 'efficient contented progressive workmen and women' who would prosper and improve themselves in such a setting. Spirella had grown successful on the introduction of metal, rather than whalebone, springs within the elaborate engineering of women's stays and was a fast-growing company, despite the threat posed to their product by rational dress and independently minded women. Eager that their employees should have 'right thoughts, right methods of living, right methods of work, an appreciation of the vital needs of sunlight, of wholesome food for health, and of congenial employment for happiness', the company considered Letchworth an ideal location for its new venture.

Having set up in temporary premises in 1910, Spirella quickly commissioned their own factory from Cecil Hignett, who had worked in the office of the architect planners of the Garden City, Parker and Unwin. The factory was built in three phases between

An early postcard depicting the 'Factory of Beauty', the Spirella Company corset factory, 1912–22, Letchworth Garden City, Hertfordshire, architect Cecil Hignett.

1912 and 1920, a process much extended by the First World War. Hignett's building was fronted by a pair of handsome tiled hipped-roofed buildings, an Arts and Crafts image that was designed to belie the fact that much of the structure behind was of reinforced concrete. Creeper-clad and set in well-maintained gardens, the setting was almost arcadian. Inside the *corsetières* worked at benches that were flooded with light, pouring down through leaded windows, set between mullions and transoms of cast concrete. With so many backward glances the building was inevitably, but affectionately, nicknamed Castle Corset, though the company preferred to call it 'the Factory of Beauty'. Spirella's harmonious dress and architectural good manners showed that the new model factory could sit down in any company.

By the time that the much admired and functionally purposeful Shredded Wheat factory, probably the single most faithful homage to the aesthetic of the North American grain silo to be built in Britain, appeared by the railway tracks in Welwyn Garden City in 1925, it could be claimed that 'a factory belt has no terrors, since the absence of smoke gives an industrial building the chance of being a feature in the landscape'. Designed by Louis de Soissons, the joint master-planner of Ebenezer Howard's second Garden

Arts & Crafts detail expanded to appropriate scale in the Spirella corset factory, one of the earliest to be built in Ebenezer Howard's first Garden City.

City, it was self-evidently a factory for a new era. Electricity and the internal combustion engine allowed reassuring new models to replace the dark mills and the *faux*-palaces of nineteenth-century industrialization.

By 1930 there were almost 7,000 manufacturing jobs in Letchworth.[2] The Garden Cities became exemplars of low-density planning and conscientious zoning, but also of a fresh architectural outlook that was at times surprisingly progressive – setting the scene for the ambitious New Town programme that developed in post-war Britain.

Trafford Park, close to the Manchester Ship Canal, dated from 1896. Like Letchworth, it was a harbinger of a new breed, in its case the trading estate that stood at a distance from the expanding centres of heavy industry at major ports and, for that matter, from the degraded fabric of recently industrialized cities. The greenfield industrial estate, with work and home only a short train or tram ride apart, was the pointer to planning orthodoxies to come.[3] Trafford Park, which had once been a country estate, became the western gateway to the United Kingdom for dozens of American companies breaking into the European market, beginning with Westinghouse in 1902. In 1911 came Ford, soon to be joined by the Trussed Concrete Steel Company (Truscon), marketing a system of concrete reinforcement patented by Julius Kahn in 1903.

It was oddly appropriate that this company should set up at Trafford Park. A business that was spearheading the introduction of industrialized construction, best suited to factory buildings, had located in a trading estate that represented the very vanguard of new ideas. The conjunction of American industrial innovation with European planning and organization was to be a highly significant moment.

First Gropius and then, some years later, Le Corbusier published images of North American grain stores and elevators, citing them as impeccably functional buildings. These plates are from *Vers une architecture* (1923).

The silos of the Shredded Wheat factory, Welwyn Garden City, Hertfordshire, c. 1925, architect Louis de Soissons. American companies were among the first to move to the new Garden Cities.

In 1917 Moritz Kahn, Julius Kahn's brother, who had already established Truscon in London in 1907, published *The Design and Construction of Industrial Buildings* in order, he wrote, to answer the question that architects so often asked their structural engineers: how to build 'efficient factories'. He also had a product to sell, the so-called Kahn Daylight System, soon to be known simply as 'The Model Factory', the prototype of which was the new Ford plant at Highland Park, Detroit, designed by yet another brother, the architect Albert Kahn.

Kahn advised manufacturers to spend time visiting the best and most representative plants, interviewing owners and consulting architects, but factories 'should look like what they are – factories and nothing else'. It was essential to look ten years ahead and use standardized units for possible expansion. 'The ideal plant is like an expanding library made up of sectional bookcases', he wrote. The example of flexibility that he chose to illustrate was Albert Kahn's building of 1905 for Packard in Detroit, Building No. 10, the first to use the Kahn reinforced concrete system successfully, which had been effortlessly extended by an additional two storeys in 1911.

Flexibility quickly became the objective of much twentieth-century architecture, but nowhere more so than in the workplace. Changing working practices were continually affecting the factory. The industrial-building envelope had already been transformed by the huge spinning frames and steam engines of second-generation textile mills, a web of overhead shafts conveying the power to the machines below. In America, standardization of parts, borrowed from small-arms manufacture, had become common. Now working procedure was also to be subject to rational rearrangement. Increased efficiency, higher productivity and lower prices followed.

The Ford magneto plant, set up in 1913 at Highland Park, was the first in the world to be arranged around a continuous moving assembly line. As a result, the time spent putting together the chassis of the Model T Ford fell from twelve-and-a-half hours to well under three. Each group of operatives performed a familiar and specific task or tasks. Systems of scientific management as advocated by the mechanical engineer Frederick 'Speedy' Taylor, and the study of action (time and motion) that had been recorded photographically by his followers Frank and Lillian Gilbreth, led to efficient, if tedious, working patterns that would determine the plan and form of the early twentieth-century factory.[4] The changes at Highland Park also led to the introduction of the eight-hour day and the $5 daily wage, with profit-sharing.

To house these reorganized activities, Moritz Kahn identified three types of industrial building: a single-storeyed roof-lit model (he showed a Rhode Island weaving shed with a sawtoothed roof); a variant with long-span roof trusses and overhead travelling cranes; and the multi-storeyed factory, the cheapest option, which was suitable for light products or wherever land was expensive or restricted. He cautioned against the use of stone, which gave 'an

The workforce changing for the 4 o'clock shift, Ford Motor Company, Highland Park, Detroit, Michigan, 1910s. Albert Kahn's factory, its layout guided by the principles of scientific management, runs the full length of the block to the left.

Main frontage of the Highland Park factory. An early and highly influential example of the 'daylight factory' (1910s), and the birthplace of new and efficient working practices.

effect of dreariness and general depression within the building', and suggested a skeleton of structural steelwork and fireproof floors, with metal windows and infill panels of brick or concrete. Yet Kahn was surprisingly downbeat about the material he championed. 'One should not . . . be carried away by those reinforced concrete enthusiasts who believe that this material is equally well suited to all forms of building'. It had its limitations and could be ugly. A pleasing elevation, be it just an ornamental cornice, would, he considered, affect the employees' mental attitude to their work and offer 'great advertising value' – for every image of the factory in a newspaper, catalogue or advertisement makes an impression.

The prefabricated factories that left the Victorian foundries of Manchester and Millwall to be shipped out to India, Turkey or Sweden were the foot-soldiers in this march of standardization, an international style that followed in the steps of world trade. From all over the industrialized world, manufacturers came to observe Henry Ford's empire and copy its working practices. The earliest visitors to Detroit were the big men of the infant European car industry, but after the war any and every enterprising industrialist took the trail to Michigan. As late as 1950 the Japanese engineer Eiji Toyota headed for Ford's River Rouge plant, but now in order to learn from the deficiencies of the old approach. As a result, Japanese cars were soon being assembled in half the time, at higher quality and in half the space.[5] Two more decades would see executives from the leading European and American car manufacturers making the pilgrimage to Japan, to learn the lessons offered there.

In Europe, the Fiat Lingotto factory in Turin was the earliest and most faithful architectural rendering of Highland Park, designed from 1915 onwards by the company engineer Giacomo Matte' Trucco in stated admiration of Albert Kahn's work in Detroit.

Neatly contained in the form of two massive courtyards, corralled at rooftop level by a cambered loop of test track a full kilometre in length, the Fiat Lingotto itself rapidly achieved fame as an apparently entirely functional work of architecture. The gradually assembled car body journeyed through and up the building – the Model Ts at Highland Park were assembled conversely, top to bottom – until the completed vehicle drove its test lap, victoriously, on the roof. Triumphantly, the Italians heralded their successful reinterpretation of the American model: such a 'bold Italian design will henceforth be an example to American industry'.[6] From widely different political viewpoints, national pride was felt to be extremely well served by the dynamic symbolism of the Lingotto rooftop.

By the 1920s Albert Kahn's Detroit practice had become the largest in the world, employing around 400 people. Affected by the models of manufacturing organization, technical innovation and building procurement with which Kahn and his colleagues were by now so familiar, the office was a place for technicians, not designers. Kahn avoided hiring architectural graduates, believing that

The Fiat Lingotto roof with its testing track in action, as published by Le Corbusier in *Vers une architecture* to illustrate the fusion of engineering, speed and clean structure.

they would tend to 'place self-expression over team co-operation'.[7]
His competition came from the Austin Company in Cleveland,
Ohio, which since 1914 had been offering standardized steel-
framed sheds for all eventualities, a design and build package that
was dignified as 'The Austin Method of Undivided Responsibility'.
Austin provided ten versions of the shed, with interchangeable

An aerial view of the rooftop of the Fiat factory, Lingotto, Turin, completed c. 1919,
engineer Giacomo Matte' Trucco. The steeply cambered turns were challenging to
negotiate at speed.

roofs, spans and fenestration, which were, demonstrably, the economic and practical answer to many manufacturers' needs.

At the Ford works at River Rouge, Dearborn, Michigan, which was now competing with Highland Park as the nerve centre of the Ford operation, ideas of scientific management and of manufacturing self-sufficiency were sweeping all before them. Albert Kahn's expertise lay both in the master-planning of a complex chain of interconnected processes on a quite massive scale, starting with the iron ore and finishing with the vehicles, and in the design of numerous highly specialist key buildings. The Glass Plant of 1922 and the Open Hearth steel mill of 1925 were both structures determined by the need to generate and disperse extremes of temperature, architecturally expressed in cigarette-thin chimneys and the tough and repetitive forms of horizontal louvres. The new plant and the new Model A Ford were celebrated in an energetic publicity campaign that included a photographic commission for the painter and photographer Charles Sheeler. His six weeks at the Rouge plant in late 1927 resulted in a series of heroic architectural images that were widely published, ensuring that the latest phase of collaboration between Ford and Kahn was soon as internationally well known as the earlier work.[8]

Henry Ford's pursuit of overseas trade soon led him to the Soviet Union and to the coining of a new term, 'Fordismus', for his approach. 'Fordism is a system the principles of which have been known for long, [having been] laid down by Marx' was the surprising conclusion of the editors of a Russian translation of Henry Ford's *My Life and Works* in the early 1920s, while Stalin quite simply considered Ford the 'greatest industrialist in the world'. Aldous Huxley's *Brave New World* (1932) would paint a futuristic world in which Ford was the deity and 'By Ford' the appropriate profanity. In the real word Stalinism met Fordism, to extraordinary effect.

By 1928, the year of the inauguration of the USSR's first Five Year Plan ('the Great Leap Forward'), a Ford Tractor plant was commissioned as the key element within the industrial zone at Stalin's new city on the Volga, Stalingrad. Soviet planners visited Detroit, and once the deal was settled it was obvious to Ford that Kahn's firm would be the people for a project on this scale. Moritz Kahn travelled to Russia with a team from the Detroit office to train a design bureau of some 4,500 architects, engineers, designers and technicians. Between 1928 and early 1932 construction of more than 500 industrial plants was set in motion – steelworks, aeronautical and automobile factories, chemical plants and more. With the Depression, these projects were invaluable for Kahn's office. Not surprisingly, the Austin

The power house of the Ford Motor Company's River Rouge plant, Dearborn, Michigan, 1941, architect Albert Kahn. The stacks were the most visible element of the factory in the landscape, a lean and gleaming image of industry.

company was also actively involved in the Soviet Union over these years.

The early Soviet factories were prefabricated from materials imported from the USA. Difficulties with skills and supply meant continual frustration in the completion of the programme in a half-forgotten, paradoxical episode of confluence between capitalism and communism. At home in the USA, public opinion turned against the experiment, fearful that these buildings might quietly be converted into munitions factories, but Intourist still offered the readers of *Fortune* magazine tours of Soviet industrial developments alongside the Kremlin and other, more traditional, monuments. In March 1932 Kahn and his team left, but their designs and technical expertise remained behind. Ironically enough, many of the factories were indeed put to new uses for

Interior of Kahn's tool and die building, Ford River Rouge plant, Dearborn, 1941, the scale of which reduces workers to ants.

The Stalinsk steel plant, USSR, c. 1936, a heroic image of Soviet industrialization, much of it (typically) brought into being by American building professionals.

armament manufacture, but in a war that found the Americans and the Soviets on the same side.

Fordismus, as expressed by Kahn's system-built factories, offered replicable forms and procedures and was highly appropriate to centralized rational planning and central authority. It seemed a mirror of technology itself, against which the painstaking efforts of any purpose-built design were bound to founder, as the difficulties that attended the building of Erich Mendelsohn's non-standardized Red Flag Textile plant at Leningrad, and which caused him to distance himself from the whole enterprise, amply illustrate.

At the same time, the Depression in the American economy left many of the most vociferous European admirers of Ford and Taylor deeply disillusioned. Their new systems had offered almost utopian promise, but were now revealed, equally simplistically, to lie at the root of the collapse of capitalism. Le Corbusier turned virulently on what he had formerly viewed as a liberating mechanistic model.

Blithely regardless of shifts of opinion among intellectuals and artists, Albert Kahn and Henry Ford continued to expand their operations, as circumstances demanded. The zenith, in terms of scale at least, was the Ford works at Willow Run, Michigan, where Second World War B-24 bombers were manufactured in 'the most enormous room in the history of man', an immense space that was 'horizontally, what the Empire State Building is, vertically, to American industry and architecture', as a reporter in the *Christian Science Monitor* described it. The building was a greater success than the planes: production problems led to the plant's being nick-named 'Will it Run?'. Yet Kahn's Glenn Martin aeroplane plant in Baltimore, which had been constructed in an astounding eleven weeks using bridge-building techniques, achieved even more attention when Ludwig Mies van der Rohe celebrated its immense, clear interior as the setting for his collage *Concert Hall* of 1942, giving no credit to Kahn (who died that year). In the real world, the only challenge to the supremacy of Albert Kahn Inc. was the development by the Austin Company of the 'windowless factory', fully air conditioned and blacked-out for wartime production. The Consolidated Vultee bomber plant at Fort Worth, Texas, in 1942 boasted an assembly area more than one kilometre in length.

But not all revolutions in working practice and manufacture were carried out on so gigantic a scale. In 1904 Tomás Bata, a small shoe manufacturer with immense ambitions, went with two shoemakers and a machinist to America. With the experience he had gained from working on an assembly line there, and the lessons he had learnt from northern German industrial expansion, Bata rapidly transformed his business in Zlín, Moravia, from an artisan enterprise to a highly productive, mechanized one. At the outbreak of the First World War he was well positioned to fulfil major contracts for military footwear.

With peace, Tomás Bata headed back to the USA, to Michigan, eager to see for himself the latest development at Ford's River Rouge plant, which was already promising to eclipse the Highland Park works, itself operational for little more than a decade. Although Bata was inspired by the way in which the vast new complex was designed around a continuous flow, from raw material to end product, he was not impressed by the company policy towards its workers.

What did strike a chord with Bata was Henry Ford's growing interest in so-called village industries, spreading manufacture across a far-flung network of smaller works. From its roots in remote Moravia, Tomás Bata's own experiment turned rapidly into a global enterprise, assisted by the devaluation of the Czech currency, and based on a far more wholehearted and progressive version of decentralization than Ford would ever achieve.[9]

Bata instigated an autonomous system that he had borrowed from the optical firm of Carl Zeiss, in which workers were grouped into departmental units, competing with one another towards targets, their success measured in their wage packets. Self-management and self-respect were core values within the company. With the post-war explosion in the market for inexpensive, machine-made footwear, Bata was eager to find a suitable factory building type and a system to build and replicate it. He set himself up as his own contractor and looked carefully at the ideas of Ebenezer Howard and the Garden City experiment, so that his workers could live in pleasant company towns. The 'factory in the garden' would be surrounded by a chessboard of detached houses, each with their own plot of land. The employees at Zlín were country people, and the atmosphere in the company town was based on Tomas Báta's belief in participation and opportunities for all his workers, regardless of status.

Remnants of the old Zlín, Moravia, Czech Republic, reduced to Lilliputian scale by the new Bata industrial complex in the distance. Photograph 1937.

For the factories, 50 alone at Zlín, Bata insisted on a replicable system based on what he had observed in the USA. The town architect, Frantisek Gahura, with an architect–engineer colleague, Arnost Sehdal, adopted a standardized system of a modular concrete skeleton, with columns and infill panels of brick, glass or steel. Aerial conveyor belts linked each production unit and measured output. From 1930 the Bata company's international architect-in-chief was Vladimir Karfík, who had worked with both Frank Lloyd Wright and Le Corbusier.

Tomás Bata articulated his aspirations. 'It would not be difficult to create a town with 50,000 people huddled in the barracks or tenement houses . . . Our aim is to build a garden town, full of sunshine, water and green grass – a clean town with the highest of wages, prosperous . . . with the best of schools.'[10] Women would be freed from 'the last traces of physical labour' and children would grow up in the best available conditions. Moritz Kahn had written that no state could allow (or afford) a factory to be 'an institution without a soul' for 'no trouble is too great and no expense unwarranted, which leads to the perfect result – ie the greatest possible efficiency of output combined with the greatest possible convenience and comfort for the workers'. Eva Jiřicna, the distinguished London-based architect, was born in Zlín, where her father, Josef Jiřicny, began work in 1938 as architect in charge of exhibitions and shop design – responsible, in effect, for the wider public face of Bata. She recalls the impressive modernity of every aspect of the environment, from her nursery school to the comfortable houses linked by a network of footpaths to the central areas.

Between 1922 and Tomás's tragic death in an air crash in 1932, the company expansion was phenomenal. In Zlín, 36 million pairs of shoes per year were being made, one third for export, in the

'Detroit of Czechoslovakia'.[11] After Bata's death, a replica of the plane in which he had died was enshrined in a glass mausoleum in Zlín. Designed as a wholly transparent 'display cabinet', it stood at the heart of the town, a bright reminder of the extraordinary man behind the Bata empire. His half-brother Jan continued the work, and in some locations entire 'mini-Zlíns' were developed.

In 1937 Karfik built a multi-storey administration block in Zlín. At one corner of the tower was an air-conditioned, glass-walled lift, large enough for Jan Bata to use as his office and in which he hovered above the heads of his staff, able to check on their progress or descend to their respective levels for meetings as required. Like the Director's house at Ledoux's Saline de Chaux, the upper chamber of the Panopticon or W. H. Lever's own office-lift at Port Sunlight, it constituted an all-seeing eye.

The Bata experiment, so ambitious and ever-expanding, appealed to the modernists for its potential. In 1935 Karfik had invited Le Corbusier to judge an international competition for workers' housing, and asked him to draw up schemes for two sites, one near Zlín and one in France. Le Corbusier imagined that he had

General view of Zlín, Moravia, with housing and industry developed by Tomás Bata, seen before 1937.

found the perfect test-bed for his ideas of the linear city and the *usine verte*, but he had reckoned without the enduring legacy of Tomás Bata's ideas, with their emphasis on the family, individuality and the physical model of the Garden City. Nor did Le Corbusier's *dirigiste* personality attune well with the ethos of the company.[12] Only after nationalization, and wartime bombing, did multi-storey housing begin to appear at Zlín, borrowing elements from the pre-war Corbusian plan.[13]

Bata had expanded globally, stretching from Europe to South Africa, India, Egypt, Singapore and the United States. The company towns wore their identity with pride: there was Bataville in France, Batanagar in India and Batapur in post-partition Pakistan. The company remained family owned, and continued to pursue Bata's ideals about working conditions, until the annexation of Czechoslovakia in 1938. The Bata family split and the company

The 1933 glass-built memorial to Tomás Bata at Zlín (architect F. L. Gahura), which incorporates a piece of the plane in which he had been killed in 1932. Currently under restoration.

became a political football, while Tomás's son, Thomas J. Bata, moved what he could of the business to Batawa in Canada. Now, with the enthusiastic support of the Bata family for the development of the Tomás Bata University at Zlín, Eva Jiřicna has been asked to design a multi-purpose auditorium and library. The wheel has come full circle.

In almost every location, the establishment of a Bata factory meant the development of a planned industrial village. The British enterprise began at East Tilbury in Essex, opening the year after Tomás's death, using an adapted version of the module construction system developed at Zlín. The town centred on three five-storey factory buildings, one for leather, one for textiles and the third for administration. This was a very reduced version of the original plan, which envisaged twelve factories, three of which were to be ten storeys high. A hotel and housing followed. Belatedly bringing Czech modernism to Essex soil, the Bata village was an imperfect but intriguing experiment.

Huge enterprises such as Ford or Bata had utter clarity of objective, initially set by the vision of a single autocratic individual, which drove the entire exercise and determined almost every detail of the outcome. Ford had elevated the machine high above the man, but Bata had, extraordinarily, come close to inverting the order. In the immediate post-war years in Britain, factory building suffered the severe repercussions arising, in the view of two experienced practitioners, from the 'lack of philosophy to order and integrate manufacturing, society and the environment as a whole'.[14]

The story of the Brynmawr Rubber Plant in South Wales demonstrated precisely this weakness, even as its foundation exemplified praiseworthy aspirations. Social concern and progressive architecture were not sufficient to carry out a commercially uncertain project. Lord Forrester's venture was a heroic tragedy of good intentions. As Andrew Saint put it neatly, 'never surely can such a tangle of idealism, effort, sophistication and sheer folly have come together in a building project'.[15]

Forrester's object was to build a model factory for rubber products in economically depressed South Wales. It would be a highly engineered shed, combining elegance and practicality, offering employment in an area long suffering from the contraction of traditional heavy industries, especially iron working and coal mining, in every respect well distanced from the unattractive scene of Victorian and inter-war industrial Britain. Forrester derided 'the new industrial hotchpotch of Park Royal, Castle Bromwich, East Moors or Coventry [which] is little more appetising than the old . . . The Lancashire mill, towering above the wretched homes that surround it, is perhaps less blameworthy than the neo-Egyptian colossus flanking some arterial roads on the outskirts of a great city.'[16] He could also have cited the grim shadows thrown by the fortified round towers of the Nantyglo ironworks, in the next village to Brynmawr, which had been built between 1816 and 1822 by repressive English iron masters in an effort to bring their desperate and rioting workers under control.[17]

In marked contrast, the Brynmawr factory, designed by the Architects' Co-operative Partnership (later known as the Architects' Co-Partnership) and planned and built between 1946 and 1951, offered a symbolic vision of modernity and optimism, with its rippling sequence of concrete parabolic vaults seen over the fields and rooftops, a beacon of progressive thinking. It immediately became a point of pilgrimage for architectural students and was published around the world. The model was proudly displayed at the Festival of Britain of 1951.

Initial development had been encouraged by a generous government subsidy, and the site was a newly designated Trading Estate,

but the timing, immediately after the war and in the teeth of continued rationing of materials, was neither auspicious nor practical. Finally completed, it turned out to have cost twice the original estimate and to be fatally inflexible. Nevertheless, Lord Forrester was enormously proud of his factory: 'he would put machines in the windows to encourage passing people to call in. If anybody wanted to see the building he would spend the whole day taking them round'.[18] More fatal still, management was haphazard and marketing uncertain. In late 1952, after just one year of production, the enterprise failed. A year later it was rescued by Dunlop. Early in 1982 Dunlop closed down the operation. After years of dereliction, and despite its listing as a pioneering example of the use of shell concrete, underpinned by a strenuous campaign to save it, the factory was finally demolished in the early summer of 2001.

The Brynmawr Rubber Plant, South Wales, interior photograph showing the structural grid, each section marked by a concrete parabolic dome. Natural light and colour were used to enliven the workplace. 1945–51, Architects' Co-Partnership, engineer Ove Arup.

In immediately pre- and post-war Europe, there was a new emphasis on functional precedent, a new kind of model. James Richards's *The Functional Tradition* (published in 1958, but based on earlier articles in the *Architectural Review* and investigations by Richards and John Piper in the 1930s) made the case that the prototypal industrial buildings of the early nineteenth century had also prepared modern taste for their successors. Using Eric de Maré's sternly beautiful black and white photographs, the co-authors celebrated the 'pioneer efforts of the engineers' as of the more orthodox builders of their time, who served the needs of farmers, millers, brewers, mariners and nautical men, textiles manufacturers and the rest with quiet effectiveness. The celebrated early iron structures, Richards argued, had become 'reflected in the mirror of our own interest in history. What their contemporaries saw as objects, we saw as images, with the result that their merits sometimes became distorted'. Now seeking consolidation after innovation, he felt that the latest generation of architects might with advantage aim at the perfection of 'such a vernacular'.

In reality, the favoured vernacular was imported. 'Prestige pancakes', as the *Architects' Journal* later termed them, were built on greenfield sites, elegant slivers of building set down into well-designed landscape, following the much admired American pattern set by Eliel Saarinen and his son Eero for General Motors at Warren, Michigan, immediately after the war.[19] Often the companies were themselves American and sometimes the architects too.

From the 1950s the Cummins Diesel Engine Company, encouraged by a board member, J. Irwin Miller, had made a notable commitment to architectural patronage in its home town, Columbus, Indiana. The firm, and later the Foundation in its name, subsidized an astonishing range of public buildings by noted architects in the town, with the view that 'it is expensive to be mediocre in this world',[20] and ensured that their own facilities matched this high standard. Harry Weese remodelled the manufacturing plant in 1961 and added a Technical Centre a few years later. In 1973 Kevin Roche and John Dinkeloo built the Components Plant. Tens of thousands of visitors poured to Columbus to see the results, and overseas the company followed a similar policy of seeking the highest standards and best quality in anything that bore its name.

Thus Cummins' factory of 1966 in Darlington, Co. Durham, was evidence of everything that was best in American industrial architecture. Kevin Roche and John Dinkeloo, inheritors of Eero Saarinen's practice, here introduced the UK to Cor-Ten weathering steel and neoprene gaskets (a way of fixing glazed panels), the latter being used internally, too, for the first time anywhere in the world. Physical demarcations between factory floor and offices were dissolved, a transforming example in British factory design. The grassy setting and reflective lake harked back to the high landscape standards set by its American peers. In the late 1970s the British architectural practice of Ahrends Burton and Koralek rose to the challenge of a Cummins commission, this time at Shotts, in Scotland.[21]

Always with an eye on the USA, clean lines and sleek cladding materials became the face of industrial modernity and provided an elegant corporate identity. In Britain the Horizon cigarette factory designed for John Player and the IBM assembly plant at Havant, Hampshire, both designed by Arup Associates in the early 1970s, were among the best of the British examples of these svelte single-storey complexes or 'cool boxes'. The model began to set the norm, from industrial estate to business park.

Inside much was changing. 'Group technology' meant that teams of workers took full responsibility for the entire process, introduced

The interior of Cummins Engine Co. factory, Darlington, Co. Durham, showing the scale and high degree of mechanization in the huge American-owned and designed factory. 1966, architects Roche, Dinkeloo & Associates.

Cummins Engine Co. factory, Darlington, aptly illustrating how the term 'prestige pancake' fitted the best of a new generation of American-inspired factories.

to combat the numbing boredom of the assembly line. The latter was best left to robot mechanics. Flexibility was the mantra, and the apparent structural adaptability of those industrial sheds that exposed services and major components of the building to view suggested that High Tech, dependent on highly engineered, light-weight structures, might offer the answer. In reality, the key iconic buildings proved to be short-lived or disappointingly inflexible in the face of unforeseen and changing requirements. The new industrial aesthetic was an image, rather than a reality.

By 1980 *Design* magazine considered that the 'innovatory period of the 'sixties and 'seventies is coming to an end. Today kit-of-parts buildings designed by one-time young lions . . . are, if not commonplace, certainly part of current conventional wisdom'. The attraction of the factory as a formulaic building type meant that 'legions of disciples have adopted the same approach, not always with happy results'.[22] From one point of view, the model was already showing all the signs of becoming an architectural cliché, while from a populist point of view it flourished and could be viewed as a legitimate modern vernacular, the 'Big Shed' that com-bines 'perfect formal simplicity with a wonderful sophistication'.[23]

4 Factory as Innovator

As soon as we know how to use the material which industry supplies us with we shall be able to create an architecture of our own.
Theophile Gautier, 1850[1]

The history of invention and innovation is imprinted with the faint shadows of those who hesitated and lost their moment, as well as those who moved too fast. Some years after the fire at the Albion Mill in London, that most public failure, the elderly James Watt admitted that the project had been too ambitious. 'It was', he said, 'too great, too new'.

Almost a century before, in the 1720s, while making a lengthy tour of Great Britain, Daniel Defoe was stopped in his tracks as he crossed the River Derwent at Derby by a newly built silk mill, 'a curiosity in trade worth observing', since its water wheel was powering machinery. The water wheel was hardly a novelty, but the scale of the building and the way in which the manufacture was being carried out were quite new. Defoe observed that the mill produced no handmade items, 'yet it turns the other work, and performs the labour of many hands. Whether it answers the expense or not, that is not my business.'[2]

The austere five-storey mill, built by John Lombe in 1717, was probably the first mechanized factory in the world, and its advances were based on Lombe's observations of Italian silk manufacture. A single water wheel of heroic proportions drove the thicket of winding and twisting machines overhead. Yet an almost 50-year interval fell between the establishment of Lombe's mill and

the beginning of wider-scale industrial activity, based on mechanized processes of manufacture. The length of that pause is still not satisfactorily explained. But once the revolution began, 'the form of the shell of the archetypal mill grew logically from internal forces like a soap bubble'.[3]

Once the steam engine entered the picture there was no longer any need to site factories close to waterfalls or for them to be entirely dependent on the vagaries of wind and weather. Location was dictated by proximity to the supply of essential materials and ease of distribution. Those northern cities in Britain served by canals and, soon after, railways answered the need. The introduction of the hard, bright light of coal gas meant that floor size could be dramatically increased, matching the expanding size and weight of the looms. Long, low buildings were needed instead of squat,

The Lombe brothers' silk mill at Derby, 1717–19. The engineer George Sorocold had already built a smaller version, but this is the one described by Daniel Defoe in the early 1720s.

high ones; the search was on for a roof form that would allow natural top lighting.

The first wave of new industrial enterprises was pioneering too in matters such as time-keeping, quality control, safety, careful bookkeeping and cleanliness, those overt indicators of orderliness and efficiency, while, necessarily, working practice was to be a major determinant of the physical planning of the factory floor. As early as the 1760s, at Josiah Wedgwood's Etruria pottery in Staffordshire, the linear arrangement of the works mirrored the sequence of production, while careful consideration was given to optimizing sources of natural light in areas where wheels and lathes were operated.[4]

At their Soho Foundry in Birmingham, built in 1796, Matthew Boulton and James Watt, makers of the first steam engines, developed the benefits of 'a definite systematic and preconceived plan'.[5] This was in marked contrast to Boulton's and John Fothergill's Soho Manufactory built thirty years before, which more closely resembled a sizeable country house, an appropriate enough image for a works given to the production of silver plate and domestic ornamental objects.

But the ultimate challenge was to build an invulnerable, fire-proof, mill. A multi-storeyed building lit by banks of candles or by oil lamps was an inevitable fire risk, since spilled wax built up under foot and continuous oil leaks saturated the floors, while inflammable waste materials and wooden machinery waited nearby to fuel the flames. The tendency of water power to fail in periods of drought or harsh frost meant even longer hours in which exhausted workers struggled to make up production targets under artificial light, with the increased risk of accident. Being held to ransom by fire or water was in the nature of the manufacturer's life.

William Strutt, the engineer son of Jedediah Strutt, was deter-mined to crack the problem. The solution seemed to him to lie in the use of brick or hollow pots to replace timber and the intro-duction of lighter and more tensile wrought-iron tie-rods to strengthen the fabric. At their pioneering Derby mill of 1792–3, the Strutts introduced cast-iron columns (already used in churches) to support a brick frame and encased the wooden beams in plaster. The structure was repeated at a larger scale for their enormous Belper West Mill, begun in 1793.[6] The urgency of their quest was regularly underlined by mill fires, at least five occurring within an 80-kilometre radius of Derby in the 1790s. Between 1795 and 1843 the cost of factory, warehouse and mill losses by fire were estimated to amount to some £2,250,000, much of it met by the insurance companies.

In 1796 a new flax mill opened in Shrewsbury, Shropshire. A local newspaper celebrated the completion of the first building in the world to use cast iron for both columns and beams: 'Messrs

The Etruria pottery, Hanley, Stoke-on-Trent, Staffordshire, an early attempt to design a symmetrical and architecturally coherent factory. Built in 1769 by architect Joseph Pickford and his clients Josiah Wedgwood and Thomas Bentley. Viewed in the 1770s by Stebbing Shaw.

Benyon & Bage . . . have just finished a spacious Flax-spinning Mill, which is *fire-proof*. The materials consist wholly of brick and iron; the floors being arched, and the beams and pillars being formed of cast iron.' William Strutt quickly called in Charles Bage to build North Mill, Belper, Derbyshire (1803), along the same lines. He also improved working conditions by using the steam that powered the machinery to heat the building, via the iron columns.

Within a small circle, initially that of men based around Coalbrookdale and the textiles centres of the Midlands and the Pennines, iron masters shaded into mechanical engineers, mechanical engineers into builders, builders into architects and developers. Word passed around among them, publications and learned papers circulated, one man's experiment became the next man's investment.[7]

The Strutts' continual alertness towards new and improved structures also led to their adoption of a version of the Panopticon, in the form of a polygonal textiles mill at Belper built between 1803 and 1813.[8] Bentham, in his publication of 1791, had extended his plan for workhouses and prisons to factories organized on the 'ordinary plan of freedom'. He had emphasized the practicality of partitions (which at Belper became firescreens), as well as the need for supervision. At Belper, this came from an overseer who sat upon a revolving central upper chamber, driven by wind or hand as the conditions allowed. The Strutts' round building did not fall victim to fire, but neither was it practical, either for machinery or workforce. (Round or polygonal buildings did, however, have their uses; it was a form that came into its own for the assembly of heavy items, such as pianos, which could be rolled down ramps.)

Of all materials, iron was the key to the century of transformation, 1750 to 1850. The engineer and historian James Sutherland points out that the Industrial Revolution could equally well be called the Iron Revolution.[9] The continuing refinement of iron, in particular rolled sections, and the next revolutionary introduction, that of cheap mass-produced steel, were driven on by the rapid spread and development of the railway network. Although the steel-making processes invented by Henry Bessemer, William Siemens and others in the 1850s and '60s did not bear fruit until the 1880s, its potential was already clear. Meanwhile, ship- and bridge-building suggested ways of greatly augmenting lengths and spans in ironwork, while railway stations, exhibition halls and arcades offered advances in the use of iron tie-rods and trusses (replacing timber), as well as modular systems of glazing – the predecessors of the top-lit factory floor space. What would now be termed technology transfer enabled new ideas to cross frontiers, to change in scale and application, despite the fact that the journey from the engineering workshop to the construction site was often a lengthy one.

Necessity drove experiment. The naval dockyards and munitions establishments of the main European powers had been the unwitting pioneers in industrial building, both in form and technology – as they had been earlier in organized labour and production. The need for quality control and the presence of a disciplined and organized workforce, as well as the skills and innovations that were forced into being at times of war, made them ideal test-beds for the civilian world of industry. At Sheerness in Kent, one building tells the story.

The Boat Store, which 'from a distance . . . looks like an admirably crisp piece of work from the 1950s',[10] is an iron-framed structure designed by a man born in 1807. Colonel Godfrey Greene was the Director of Engineering and Architectural Works at the Admiralty from 1850 until 1864, and the building, hidden away in a secure naval dockyard – where the conversion from sail to steam

had meant an introduction to advanced technology – remained undiscovered until the mid-twentieth century. Until then, Jules Saulnier's mill, built in 1871 for Chocolat Menier at Noisiel-sur-Marne, with its turbines feeding power to the factory overhead, had been celebrated as the pioneer of this form of iron construction.[11] There, the upper storeys were supported on iron box girders, and arched roof trusses permitted uninterrupted floor space for machinery at the upper level. The building's highly decorative skin of brickwork and ceramic panels seemed at odds with the ingenious engineering within, and the radical use of iron as a structural frame.

The Sheerness Boat Store, built between 1858 and 1860, had no need of such disguise. The rigour of its external appearance was at one with the innovation of its structure, in a fashion that might have been disturbingly bald to the Victorian eye had it been in a

The proto-modernist iron-framed Boat Store, Sheerness Naval Dockyard, Kent, designed in 1858 by architect Godfrey Greene.

more accessible location. Greene dispensed altogether with load-bearing walls and, by using an iron frame (cast and wrought iron for, respectively, column and beam) and lightweight corrugated iron infill panels, he pointed the way ahead to the steel-framed, panelled sheds of late twentieth-century industry.[12] The frame system that Greene used had clear advantages over conventional construction: it was quick to build, accommodated larger windows and did not require such heavy foundations. His ingenuity lay in the application of newly formulated standard sections and better quality metalwork to the well-tried, and deservedly admired, system of timber framing that had long served dockyards and mills in the south-eastern counties of England.

Looking back almost fifty years in his memoirs, the distinguished engineer Sir William Fairbairn pointed to the most dramatic change of all. In 1814 machinery had been made entirely by

An ornamental skin disguises a pioneering use of an iron frame. The Menier chocolate factory, Noisiel-sur-Marne, 1871, architect Jules Saulnier.

hand, largely of timber, but by the mid-nineteenth century iron tool-making had itself grown into a major industry: mechanization had begat mechanization. Originally a millwright, Fairbairn's own fortunes were founded on the manufacture of steam engines, water wheels, locomotives and mill gearing, and his own foundry and factory in Manchester was widely admired for its model working system in which 'each mechanic appears to have his peculiar description of work assigned, with the utmost economical subdivision of labour'. The production line itself was under development, along with the technology.

Science and technology, so long divided by 'the anomalous separation of theory and practice', had become, in Fairbairn's view and experience, an indivisible whole. Yet his fellow engineers and architects and their clients were still failing to exploit the possibilities of cast and wrought iron in buildings. As he wrote, 'experimentalists and mathematicians have provided the knowledge; but practitioners, I fear, have in a great degree failed to avail themselves of it'.[13]

In his own search for non-combustible buildings, Fairbairn had also come 'fortuitously close', as Kenneth Frampton puts it, to inventing reinforced concrete. In Fairbairn's publication of 1854, *On the Application of Cast and Wrought Iron to Building Purposes*, he proposed a system of iron beams supporting vaults formed of sheet iron, with concrete above. Within the concrete were embedded wrought-iron tie-rods, harking back to the tie bars of an earlier generation of conventional, masonry-built mills. To put metal reinforcement within the artificial stone compound, the latter the subject of much experiment from the early nineteenth century,[14] was extraordinarily prescient. The sticking point was to provide elasticity in the material, to deal with the stresses set up by the load of conventional post-and-lintel construction and which, overlooked, would inevitably lead to cracking and probably structural collapse.

Functional timber buildings, exemplified by Courtauld's 18th-century weaving sheds at Halstead, Essex, pointed ahead to further structural innovation, particularly in naval dockyards.

The breakthrough needed came from a particular joint, invented by François Hennebique and patented in 1892. His 'monolithic joint' was relatively flexible and resistant to stress. It worked by binding together the reinforcement bars of the various horizontal and vertical members of the structure at their junction. The effectiveness of the joint meant that a reliable concrete frame was possible, although it remained awkward looking. The application of the monolithic joint to industrial buildings, reducing fire risk, vibration and cost, was obvious, and in 1895 Hennebique successfully built the Charles Six spinning mill in Tourcoing in Belgium. Two years later he and his partner Le Brun designed the first reinforced concrete building in Britain, a flour mill in Swansea in South Wales, erected by the Hennebique method. By 1900 the firm had become a huge international concern. Among the licensees for the system were the Perret brothers, one of whom, Auguste, was to exploit the architectural possibilities for concrete much further. Now the race was on, and other patents, each differentiated by the precise geometry of the system of reinforcement, were developed both in Europe and the USA.

Unlike architects, who were held back from business ventures by their professional rules of disengagement, entrepreneurial structural engineers remained at the forefront of development. The Swiss Robert Maillart had built his first concrete bridge in 1898. In 1909, now running his own company, he patented a system in which the columns appeared to flow into the lightweight floor slab via a sinuous column head or capital, an elegant, fluid solution which simplified the traditional and now irrelevant junction between post, ceiling slab, joist and beam that perpetuated the forms of wooden or metal structures. The following year Maillart built a five-storey warehouse in Zurich, the first to exemplify his 'flat slab' system.[15] There the mushroom-headed or dendriform column, pressed into shape by wooden forming boards, which left an attractive imprint, proved to be an aesthetically pleasing and efficient solution to an awkward structural conundrum. In so doing, it can be seen as an apt metaphor for the practical achievement and architectural vision achieved by such pioneering engineers, yet little acknowledged by their professional peers or, until recently, by historians. As David Billington sees it, Robert Maillart epitomizes the 'design' view of engineering as against the 'applied science' view.[16] The new forms also offered tempting possibilities for alert architects. The young Finnish architect Alvar Aalto was among the first to embrace the robust possibilities of reinforced concrete in the huge mushroom-headed columns that supported the storage cellars below the offices of the Turku newspaper *Turun Sanomat*, built in the late 1920s. Aalto's friendship with many leading international artists and critics ensured that his work was quickly appreciated (and published) well beyond Scandinavia.

The paper storage cellars at the Turun Sanomat printworks, Turku, Finland, 1927–9, architect Alvar Aalto, with reinforced concrete, mushroom-headed columns of a type pioneered years earlier by Robert Maillart.

At the beginning of the twentieth century the modern factory could be seen as the perfectly functional building, built with improved or new materials and building technology, expressive of efficient procedures and management systems, owing its plan and its form to the specific nature and organization of the industrial process. Most significantly of all, it would be powered by electricity, becoming clean, bright and pleasant. Hidden behind all this was the reality for the workforce, which had to weigh a better environment and improved pay and hours against an increasingly dehumanized routine of repetitive and unstimulating labour.

Paradoxically enough, electricity and motor vehicles, those epitomes of the new age, were often produced in steel-framed and reinforced concrete buildings constructed to the latest specification but buried beneath masonry cladding and conventional ornament. When the American architects Wallis & Goodwillie were commissioned, well before the First World War, to build the General Electrical Company's headquarters at Nela Park in Cleveland, Ohio, their first action was to set sail for England. There, they toured Salisbury, Bath and Wells and steeped themselves in early eighteenth-century architecture. They returned with a portfolio of useful details plucked from examples such as Pulteney Bridge in Bath and the Judge's House in Salisbury, as well as 'coach houses and offices of old English estates'. The brickwork was beautifully detailed, the stonework carved with care, the Engineering Laboratory was a Wrennaissance masterpiece and the 200-foot-high (60.96 m) chimney had 'a delightful entasis and Doric cap'. The architecture suggested an unimpeachable pedigree, suitably reassuring while commercial electricity was still uncharted territory.[17]

The outbreak of the First World War gave reinforced concrete systems, among them Julius Kahn's well proved and heavily promoted version, the boost needed. Owen Williams's career began in 1911 with the American Indented Bar and Concrete Engineering Company, and the following year he moved to Truscon's London office to become their chief estimating engineer, designing innumerable civil factories before turning to the massive establishments required for armaments and defence hardware during the war. In 1914 Truscon began to publish *Kahn-crete Engineering*, a bimonthly magazine that extolled the product and provided practical information, as their French competitors had done for many years. There remained a need for reassurance; as late as 1919 the *Architectural Record* was reminding its (American) readers of the early history of concrete and a series 'of most lamentable accidents. These were due to causes which those properly experienced with concrete now know how to avoid.'

Fast, economic and adaptable, reinforced concrete had become readily available at just that moment when shortages of traditional materials, the relaxation of building regulations and flexibility made its virtues most persuasive. In Britain between 1913 and 1917 the Danish practice of Christiani & Nielsen designed ranks of undisguised reinforced concrete silos and warehouses for the British Oil and Cake Mills at Erith on the Thames estuary, while in France Eugène Freysinnet had spent the war years building arms and munitions factories, glass and steelworks all to gargantuan scale driven by the urgency of the moment.

In the USA the notions of the systems engineer also came to the fore in wartime, conclusively influencing the forms and materials of industrial buildings. The ideas of Frederick Taylor, who died in 1915, had been applied to a wide range of industries, from steel to munitions, reinforced concrete to machine-tool engineering. His *Principles of Scientific Management* (1911) played a considerable part in revolutionizing the Ford manufacturing process, although it can be argued that Albert Kahn and Ernest Wilby had already established 'the typological characteristics of the modern factory' in their work for the Pierce automobile plant in Buffalo, designed from 1906, in which self-contained work cycles were housed in single-storey, steel-framed, top-lit, sawtooth-glazed buildings.[18]

At Highland Park, Detroit, a new workshop had opened on New Year's Day of 1910 for the production of the Model T Ford. It was a four-storey block, each floor being entirely un-subdivided and served by freight elevators around the perimeter. Being long and narrow, it turned out to be ideally adaptable. With sizeable extensions to the original block and reordering of the entire site to cope with the increasingly specialized nature of each operation, three years later Highland Park became the site of the world's first moving assembly line. Parts travelled past operatives on a conveyor belt, enabling them to perform a single efficient task: gravity-fed car production was dead. By 1915 a quarter of a million Model T Fords were pouring out of Highland Park annually.

The logical extension of this thinking was to integrate the entire process, from the arrival of the raw materials – coal and iron ore, in particular – to the shipping out of completed models. The huge extent of the Rouge River marshes at Dearborn, Michigan, gave Ford the opportunity for an enterprise on such an all-embracing scale, and in 1918 he set up an assembly plant for the Eagle torpedo boat. Albert Kahn's Building B was half a mile (800 metres) long. Working to the adage 'An Eagle a Day, Keeps the Kaiser Away', the labour force soon adapted to post-war manufacture of car bodies. Single-storey buildings were far less vulnerable to fire and did not suffer from vibration, while steel frames meant fast construction. Kahn's vast complex was fathered by the Pierce building of 1906, while the deployment of robotics in manufacture would be the obvious next step, since repetitive, demoralizing work and escalating labour costs combined to often explosive effect in the mid-twentieth century – as caricatured by Charlie Chaplin in his film *Modern Times* (1936), the automaton-worker even being fed by machine.

Eugène Freysinnet's hangar of 1921 at Orly airport outside Paris, its arches based on the catenary principle used by Christopher Wren on the dome of St Paul's Cathedral, demonstrated the scale and impressive dimensions that reinforced concrete could achieve in the hands of the generation of innovative and radical engineers who had risen so impressively to the imperative of war. Equally, Auguste Perret's Esders clothing factory of 1919 in Paris, with its glazed roof and clear space supported by concrete arches, transformed the notion of the top-lit workshop into a great hall. Meanwhile, Owen Williams benefited from his experience with Truscon and set up Williams Concrete Structures Ltd to market his own patent, 'Fabricrete', before being appointed the leading engineer to the British Empire Exhibition of 1924 at Wembley, where he applied his wartime experience of large-scale buildings and fast construction, gaining a knighthood at a very young age for his efforts.

The purposeful austerity of Perret's industrial work of the immediate post-war years, often combining pre-cast elements with *in situ* concrete, would be shared by his later civic commissions; for, as he put it, 'how can we build palaces, if we do not build our factories the same way?'[19] Freysinnet worked on in his search to a solution to what he termed the 'dissonant deformations' of concrete and steel, that is, their antipathy under conditions of stress. In 1928 he wound up his business partnership and began to experiment with pre-stressed concrete, inducing stresses artificially in the reinforcing rods before insertion in the concrete. His efforts were vindicated when he was brought in to deal with subsidence at the Marine Terminal at Le Havre in 1933. Pre-stressed concrete was applied as a last resort, and found to be highly effective.

From then on, pre-stressed concrete was used for almost all heavy engineering projects, dams, bridges, wind tunnels, landing strips and lighthouses. Its lightness (the concrete section could now afford to be extremely slender) and adaptability made it ideal for forming cones and parabolas – while it proved reassuringly durable. According to one leading engineer, pre-stressed concrete was 'the most revolutionary idea in twentieth century structural engineering'.[20] Post-war, the Spanish-born but Mexican-based architect Felix Candela and the Italian structural engineer Pier Luigi Nervi experimented inventively and to extraordinary effect with both *in situ* and pre-cast concrete to create complex industrial and public buildings, folding, slashing and piercing the material into cones, parabolas, tentlike roofs and swooping vaults.

Concrete vaulting and columns for the Gatti Wool Mill, Rome, 1951, engineer Pier Luigi Nervi. Elsewhere Nervi mastered spanning of large expanses with reinforced concrete, for hangars, sports stadia and exhibition halls.

Until the Second World War, the three modern materials – steel framework, reinforced concrete and glass – had offered, in Albert Kahn's words, 'a straight-forward attack of the problem' in which 'simplicity and proper respect for cost of maintenance make for a type which, though strictly utilitarian and functional, has distinct architectural merit'. For Henry Ford, the continual challenge was hyper-efficiency and super-productivity; there was no time for reflection or consolidation, for 'a thing is obsolete, no matter how good it is, the moment something better appears', as William Cameron, his public relations and spokesman, put it.[21] Thus a power plant that had cost $20 million was summarily replaced in 1937 when requirements changed.

In his book Moritz Kahn emphasized the importance of lighting quality within the factory, both 'physiologically and psychologically'. In recognition of this, long before, Matthew Boulton had insisted on whitewashing the walls of the Albion Mill, both to improve the rough interiors and to reflect more light. Kahn advocated the use of translucent upper panes and clear low ones, to alleviate the strain of continually looking at one object and to help diffuse the natural light. Although Kahn did not mention safety, it was well known that poor lighting was a major cause of industrial accidents. Since the late nineteenth century, different combinations of glazing and roofing material on single-storeyed work sheds had led to various standard roof profiles which included sawtoothed, butterfly and monitor lights.

Glass offered benefits as well as difficulties. Generous glazing led to overheating – curtains, blinds and opaque paint were quickly introduced at Walter Gropius's Faguswerk (1912–14) in Alfeld-an-der-Leine and, later, awnings – but the symbolism of a transparent building, both in terms of modernity and accessibility, was potent. In 1931 Le Corbusier was transfixed by the Van Nelle

Factory in Rotterdam, begun in 1925 and recently completed. He considered Brinkman and Van der Vlugt's work (assisted by the young Mart Stam) a notable creation of the new age. An eight-storey tower rose above the lower, curving administration building. Everything was glazed and 'open to the outside'. The company packaged foodstuffs, including tea, cocoa and coffee, and an essential message to their customers was conveyed in the cleanliness and transparency of the building. The curtain walls and diagonal conveyor belts, the mushroom columns and concrete slab floors, were all part of the visible modernity of the Van Nelle factory – as were the white ceramic wall tiles, stainless-steel handrails, rubber floors and radiators tucked beneath sill level. When Howard Robertson and the architectural photographer Frank Yerbury visited the still-incomplete building for the *Architecture and Building News* in the spring of 1930 they noted that 'the factory [had] a human atmosphere of gaiety and joy'.[22] On Tuesday and Friday evenings the lights were left on in the building, ensuring that the great glittering ship of glass became a highly visible landmark across the city. The company well knew the effect that their eye-catching, illuminated new building would have on sales.

For Owen Williams, the 300-acre (121.4 ha) greenfield site that Boots wished to develop in the late 1920s outside Nottingham, at Beeston, offered a rare opportunity to design a factory as a factory was meant to be – 'a place protected from wind and weather where things, most unnecessary, are made most efficiently'. In order to be able to keep full control of the design, he registered himself as an architect in 1930.

As so often with the leading industrial buildings of the early twentieth century in Europe, the client was American, the United Drugs Company having bought Jesse Boot's firm. The plan was to build a huge manufacturing plant in three phases. In the event the

building, known as the 'Wets', which referred to its function in manufacturing, packing and distributing pharmaceutical liquids, pastes and creams, did not expand. By the time that Boots asked Williams to design another building, the 'Drys' (for powders and tablets), the firm had returned to British ownership. The second building followed a very different brief, and discarded the glass curtain wall for a more solid masonry structure. The external image of the two buildings provides a metaphor for the cultural gulf that existed between confident Machine Age America and cautious inter-war Britain.

An early 1930s night-time view of the Van Nelle factory, Rotterdam, 1925–9, architects J. A. Brinkman and L. C. van der Vlugt. Illuminated glass-walled buildings, whether factories or department stores, were a commercial gift.

With his wide experience, a programme largely defined by the production and engineering team held no fears for Williams. As the souvenir brochure expressed it, 'as a constructional engineer free from the superficial restrictions of the fashions of the building trade, he became sensitive to the living, productive organism which is Boots'. Williams was working to a precise brief, since the client team presented him with flow lines, the optimum accommodation for each operation and the necessary linkages between the many processes. His triumphant achievement was to visualize all this within a complex of two immense atria, around which everything else revolved.

The 'Wets' was revolutionary in its scale – at 695,000 square feet (645,655.5 sq. m) it approached the scale of car factories and munitions works. The four-storeyed slab structure is supported by mushroom-headed columns spaced within a grid and wrapped by a sweep of glass and steel curtain walling. Nothing like it had been seen in Britain, and overseas only the Van Nelle factory in Rotterdam could be compared to it.

An early photograph of Boots' 'Wets' factory, Beeston, Nottinghamshire. 1930–32, architect–engineer Owen Williams. After an extensive restoration, it remains as impressive as ever and is still in working use.

The production area is illuminated from above, where an immense expanse of bull's-eye glazing forms the covering of the atria. From the beginning, everything possible was mechanized: the finished products were hoisted up to the packing department by lift and came down to the ground floor on chutes. The entire organization was linear, running south to north through the building – raw materials to finished products. The benefits of the new building enabled Boots to become the first company in the country to introduce a five-day week for its staff, with no reduction of pay.

The 'Wets', completed in 1932, was officially opened by the chairman's wife on 27 July 1933. As if she were launching an ocean-going liner, Lady Trent hurled a bottle of perfume against the wall. As a contributor to the *Manchester Guardian* wrote: 'It suggests what the factory of the future may be when architects, with the new materials now at their disposal, have further revealed their ideas of industrial design.' The 'Wets' was hailed with

An early photograph of the packing hall in Boots' 'Wets' factory. Note the shutes.

The packing hall at Boots' 'Wets' factory, seen in 2001. The shutes have gone and an enclosed ground-floor area has been added, bottom left, but there are few other major changes, 70 years on.

Boots' 'Drys' factory, Beeston, 1937–8. Owen Williams's second building on the site was a more conventional structure due, in part, to the change of ownership from American to British.

warranted journalistic hyperbole in the *Glasgow Evening News* as 'the wonder factory of the world' and an 'industrial crystal palace where thousands of men and women work in the full daylight under conditions that must be the envy of every man and woman employed in the orthodox factory'.

After extensive renovation work in the mid-1990s, the main floor area of the 'Wets' still functions much as designed, amply justifying all the claims for it and a remaining an utterly compelling architectural *tour de force*, exerting a Machine Age thrill 70 years later.[23]

Yet, despite such an occasional exception, and usually only where American business partners were involved, British industry of the inter-war period remained firmly locked into the Victorian era. In the architectural magazines of the early 1930s, strenuous advertising of products such as white reflective tiles, pale 'Midhurst white' bricks and 'Snowcrete' cement did little to brighten the picture. One report in the early 1930s reported that some 30,000 factories did not even have electric light. The pioneering Wedgwood pottery works in Etruria struggled on in the eighteenth-century premises that H. G. Wells had considered sadly run-down 60 years before. Not until the late 1930s did the company commission their new works at Barlaston from Keith Murray.

As in the previous war, the shortages and restrictions brought about by the priorities of defence and essential production during the Second World War galvanized the construction industry to experiment. In the USA the stocks of traditional materials had been exhausted by mid-1942. Steel was reserved for armaments, so that reinforced concrete and timber byproducts, such as plywood, came into their own. Despite a certain initial nervousness in the face of the unfamiliar – 'Unusual materials, designs and methods of fabrication . . . are entirely justified under prevailing conditions' – the economies and lightness of pre-stressed concrete and the dependability of columns and trusses of laminated timber turned out to be admirable. Synthetic materials, from rubber to resin glues, proved practical adjuncts to these novel building materials.[24]

After the war, the immense US defence infrastructure fell largely redundant, and Federal funding was directed, through a government agency, the Defense Plant Corporation, to the task of converting the plants to domestic industry. Aircraft engine and tank plants became car factories, notably the Willow Run bomber assembly plant at Ypsilanti, Michigan, which produced the (unsuccessful) Kaiser Frazer car before reverting to building transport planes for the Korean War.

Some plants were converted to produce industrialized buildings, in particular much-needed prefabricated housing, feeding on the over-supply of aluminium and steel. An artificial demand for newly developed materials was sustained by, for example, legislation in Congress that synthetic rubber must be used in preference to natural rubber. But the domestic market proved predictably resistant to such new products as the Lustron, an enamel-coated steel house. With peacetime and prosperity, the impetus to explore further drained away, a waste of what Martin Pawley has termed a 'temporary coincidence of science and building'.

In the USA, with the availability of ample quantities of improved quality, lightweight-steel sections, firms such as Skidmore Owings & Merrill (SOM) developed a sophisticated gridded, highly serviced shed with an exposed steel frame which, before long, was being exported to Europe for industrial use – initially on behalf of American clients. As Mies van der Rohe put it, speaking in the USA in 1950, 'Technology is far more than a method, it is a world in itself.'[25] A newly elegant reinterpretation of pre-war European modernism, evoking Gropius's and Mies's own schemes, the image, whether as architecture or as polemic, was impressive. Nevertheless, the fine steel mouldings that delineated the slender frames offered no more support than might a plaster or timber trim, since fire regulations still required much of the structural steel to be masked. In Sweden, unscathed by war or materials shortages, the British-born architect Ralph Erskine built two factories in the early 1950s (one making mattresses at Köping, the other cardboard at Östenfors), using brick in an expressive and effective way on the exteriors.[26]

The next generation of metal-framed and heavily glazed buildings were to be the beneficiaries of new sealants developed for the car industry and tougher, oxidizing steel (Cor Ten) developed for freight wagons and heavy industrial plant. Other materials, in particular reflective glazing and pre-cast concrete, also proved adaptable to 1960s industrial buildings. Further refinements,

Neutral Sweden was able to gear itself up for production earlier than many other countries in post-war Europe. In the early 1950s architect Ralph Erskine used brick in an exuberant way for this cardboard factory at Östenfors.

especially profiled steel and aluminium cladding and plastic sealants, encouraged the shed to become ever lighter, while such features as masts, cables, braces and air conditioning plant became more explicit, often celebrated in bright colours or metallic finishes, leading to what became known as High Tech.

Later twentieth-century architect-designed industrial buildings lent themselves readily to what has been termed 'architectural engineering'[27] – the use of elements that rely more on external effect than structural reality. The now-demolished but much admired Reliance Controls factory outside Swindon in Wiltshire was built at high speed in 1965 by Team 4 Architects (the practice set up by Norman and Wendy Foster and Richard and Su Rogers) – a cheap and flexible shed with strongly marked bays that served as both factory and offices for an American electronics company. Its most visually memorable feature was the crisp cross-bracing on each bay of the external steel frame. Despite the contemporary nature of the clear structural logic of the grid, the expressed frame and its light steel and glass infill panels, the designers were prepared to admit that the bracing was there just 'for visual effect'.[28]

Rather more purposefully, the masted structures at Richard Rogers's Fleetguard Manufacturing Centre at Quimper in Brittany, for American clients, the Cummins Engine Company (with Ove Arup as engineers) in 1981, and at Inmos Microprocessors at Newport, South Wales, in 1982 (with Anthony Hunt, engineers), offered flexibility, the possibility of adding prefabricated parts along a central serviced spine. The Meccano-like elements of Foster Associate's Renault depot of 1983 at Swindon emphasized the 'toys for boys' element of the overt mechanistic references. The masts, brightly coloured, helped to establish the visual impact and image for these new factories, not markedly

dissimilar from many others in France or Britain except perhaps in their aesthetic ambitions.

In fact, the sophisticated serviced shed has become a relatively standardized item. In 1980 Michael Hopkins & Partners, architects who had already shown their potential in the field of industrial buildings, were commissioned to draw up a prototype small unit. Patera, as the system was named, is a steel-framed box with glazing, a prefabricated factory unit that could nourish that enduring modernist appetite for a building that comes off the assembly line, like a car. A handful were built but there was to be no mass production.

The latest materials are probably entirely out of sight: complex combinations of resins, fibres, metals and plastics, some of which

With its clean lines and taut bracing, the Reliance Controls Electronics factory, Swindon, Wlltshire, became an influential building for an entire generation of sleek factory sheds. 1965–6, architects Team 4. Now demolished.

Masts and steel bracing rods around the building denoted new technology
at the American-owned Fleetguard Manufacturing & Distribution Centre,
Quimper, Brittany, 1979–81, architects Richard Rogers Partnership.

are replacing more traditional options, layered and sandwiched to insulate, seal and improve the environmental performance of the building. In theory, therefore, 'every building is a prototype with a choice of structure and materials'.[29]

The real innovations in the factory are equally unlikely to be visible, but hidden indoors where modern machine tools, robotics and laser technology have emptied the 'manufacturing facility' of people. Alterations in the face and pace of work, with modern ergonomic and spatial planning, have been fed into the design thinking.

Where people still remain a part of the process, a thoughtful brief and a well-considered plan can potentially change attitudes and break down hierarchies. A simple decision such as the provision of a unified canteen or a single entrance desegregates blue- and white-collar workers, improving labour relations and communications at a stroke. The Motorola factory near Swindon, built in 1998, is designed around an internal 'street', a sociable but undefined space in which employees can mingle. Sheppard Robson, the architects, have also been responsible for a number of research and development headquarters for leading biotechnological and pharmaceutical companies in Britain, arguably factories in a new guise – albeit staffed by highly qualified graduate staff. Their campus for the American pharmaceutical giant Pfizer at Walton Oaks in Surrey, opened in 2001, provides attractive, informal meeting places throughout the building, where people can swap ideas beyond the confines of office or laboratory.

Viewed in the round, a factory is not simply a well-oiled machine, nor an architectural set piece, but a complex social structure. As Jeremy Melvin writes, in a critique of the Ryder Company's exemplary Viasystems plant for printed circuit boards in North Tyneside, such a satisfactory result depends on 'the

manipulation of infrastructure, the capability for change, the understanding of different scales, and an almost ritualised regulation of the interplay between people, goods, waste and information. In short, factories are the closest phenomena to urban life . . . '.[30]

A sleek cigar of polished steel, the Motorola factory at Swindon, Wiltshire, was as mute about its function as its 'high tech' predecessors were voluble. 1998, architect Sheppard Robson.

5 Factory as Icon

... factories, the reassuring first fruits of the new age.

Le Corbusier[1]

The sense that there had to be a new approach to building, efficient, functional and unconstrained by tradition and historic style, led to an energetic search for fitting examples in the early years of the twentieth century. Logic and ideology suggested that the prototypes ought to be industrial structures – icons entirely suited to their proselytizing role.

The urgency of this mission engaged the promotional and editorial skills of a small, closely linked group of architects, photographers and critics who ensured that a selection of key buildings was widely published, each image carefully selected and, on occasion, manipulated to illustrate the point better. In fact, the *Architectural Review*'s roving editor, Philip Morton Shand, went so far as to wonder in early 1934: 'did modern photography beget modern architecture, or the reverse?'

By the time of the International Style exhibition of 1932 at the Museum of Modern Art in New York, the organizers could confidently assert that the modern factory was, at best, a perfect architectural model. 'American factories admirably illustrate how *building* is becoming more and more impersonal and scientific. The best European factories illustrate, however, that in the field of industrial construction there are real architectural possibilities.'[2]

No avant-garde group could have been more passionately engaged in the worship of new technology and contemporary processes than the Italian Futurists, yet there was scarcely an architect among them and not a single Futurist building was ever erected. In a brief interval before the outbreak of the First World War, a fringe member of the group, Antonio Sant'Elia, a 25-year-old architect, produced perspectives of subjects such as electricity generating stations, factories and airship hangars. Two years later he was dead.

Despite their opening intemperate blast against 'Big Business architecture and reinforced concrete contractors', the Futurists

Antonio Sant'Elia, study for a Futurist industrial structure, 1913.

were quick to celebrate the hurtling world of the 'great humming power station' and its 'control-panels bristling with levers and gleaming commutators' (Marinetti) as an abstract, theatrical vision. The idealization of the machine itself was inchoate and largely symbolic, expressed most tellingly in film and photography, but the search was on for an appropriate architectural model to fit the tides of polemic washing around the subject. Marinetti wasted no time in claiming the Fiat Lingotto factory as 'the first invention of Futurist construction',[3] for it was the automobile that carried the hopes of the Futurists.

Precedent and inspiration could be found in Detroit, Turin and Orly – where innovatory structures designed for the production of the motor car and the aeroplane were to be found, designed by tough-minded architects and engineers who, at the service of these new, technically driven industries, continually pushed at the frontiers of materials, forms and, above all, scale. The self-conscious father of modernist architecture, Walter Gropius, illustrated Highland Park in 1913, alongside North American grain silos and railway coal stores, as an example of the 'modern industrial hangar' that bore comparison in 'monumental force, to the constructions of ancient Egypt'. The same structures that had horrified Rudyard Kipling as he passed through Buffalo in 1889 delighted the modernists – to a man.[4] Le Corbusier would later borrow the images without attribution or acknowledgement, adding Fiat Lingotto to argue his case for an aesthetic of engineering.

Gropius's choice of models emerged from his own experience; he had already broken with precedent in his solution to the new factory. The Faguswerk in Alfeld-an-der-Leine, designed and largely completed before the outbreak of the First World War, was to become an icon, a skilfully presented image of precision and craftsmanship upon the most advanced lines. The production of beech shoe lasts, a perfect pattern for every variation of the human foot, took place in a substantially glazed building that could be demonstrated – by its clients, architects and even the contractors – to have broken the mould entirely. Intriguingly, as Annemarie Jaeggi has argued, each was exaggerating for their own ends the case for the progressive credentials of the Fagus factory, largely a masonry-built structure. But at the time it came 'nearer to an integration of the new style than any other edifice built before 1922'.[5]

Yet, ironically enough, had the rebuilding of the clicking-knife department of the Faguswerk that Gropius and his office designed between 1923 and 1925 not fallen victim to recession, there would have been an extensive glazed curtain-walled structure on the site, entirely overshadowing the earlier buildings. In 1927 the client, Carl Benscheidt Sr, acknowledged that some of Gropius's ideas had been too extreme for him and, potentially, too costly, but 'were I to build Fagus again today, I would build more extremely than I did then. Today I recognize that I would have done well to adopt more of Mr Gropius's ideas.'[6] Gropius's strenuous advancement of the Faguswerk as an iconic building implicitly included those radical unbuilt designs.

When Peter Behrens became the industrial design consultant for the Allgemeine Elektrizitäts-Gesellschaft (AEG) in 1907, he was handed the job of reconfiguring their factory complex in northern Berlin, as well as considering every other visual aspect of the enterprise, from typeface to product design. The company had taken on Edison's patents for electricity in Germany in 1883 and was in pole position to become a company of unsurpassed modernity. Yet AEG's identity was signalled by its polychrome-brick main gate, built in 1896 in the castellated Gothic Revival style beloved by northern European industrialists, with its peculiarly inappropriate imagery, harking back to candlelit great halls and the nobility. Like their

American counterparts, the directors chose to put their as yet commercially unfamiliar product in fancy dress.

By the first decade of the new century, confidence had grown and it was time to replace the ramshackle collection of factory sheds behind the fairy-tale gateway with something more appropriate. Behrens understood the potency of image, whether applied to the detail of a typeface or the larger effect achieved by the principal elevation of a building. He was neither an architect nor an engineer, but his assistant was the young architect, Walter Gropius. Other junior members of his office at this time included Mies van der Rohe and Charles-Edouard Jeanneret – after 1920 known as Le Corbusier.

The handsome dimensions and impressive structure of the Turbine Hall were designed to signal (and effect) change. The immense engines for the new centralized electricity industry were

The simple lettered tympanum and concrete rusticated plinths on Behrens's AEG gave it a monumentality that was largely an illusion.

housed in a prominent building placed gable-end on to the street, with the company name lettered on the tympanum. Here the formal essentials of the Classical temple were confidently equated with the scaled-up industrial shed. The dominant elevation masked considerable ambiguities, in particular the heavy-looking reinforced concrete pylons, which were actually of little structural use. Behrens continued to extend the huge plant behind over many years.

Behrens's and Gropius's powerful position in one of the major movements of the pre-First World War years, the Deutsche Werkbund, ensured that the AEG Turbine Hall rapidly achieved its iconic status, being published in the group's yearbook of 1913, alongside Argentinian and North American grain silos and 'daylight factories' built of reinforced concrete, all arguing for a new architecture that reflected the spirit of the age, that is, mass production.[7]

Peter Behrens, AEG (Allgemeine Elektrizitäts-Gesellschaft) factory complex, Tiergarten, Berlin, 1908 onwards. The overlay of classical elements on a rational brick core was a clear challenge to the conventional 19th-century German factory, styled in either Romanesque or Gothic Revival.

Also involved in the Werkbund was Carl Benscheidt Sr, the client for Fagus (Latin for beech), one of a number of enlightened industrialists who adhered to a socially and technologically advanced programme in their works. In 1911 his son, Karl Benscheidt Jr, worked briefly for the United Shoe Machinery Company at Beverly, Massachusetts, learning American works management in the company that was providing most of the finance for Fagus's current new development at Alfeld-an-der-Leine. The reinforced concrete daylight factory built for the company between 1903 and 1905 by the English-born agricultural engineer Ernest Ransome was currently the best known building of its type. Benscheidt may well have been the source of Gropius's photographs of American industrial buildings. Ransome's building was not among them.

Benscheidt followed the model of AEG in his approach to creating a corporate identity, but, as Annemarie Jaeggi points out, at Fagus the task was carried out collaboratively, by a group of

Clean, functional lettering on the Fagus shoe-last factory, Alfeld near Hanover, indicated a break with the past. 1911 onwards, architects Walter Gropius and Adolf Meyer.

experts, chosen and guided by the architects. Later the building would come to exemplify the objectives of the Bauhaus: colour, graphics and all furnishings were considered of a piece. The headed company stationery showed the main building set amongst sans serif lettering. 'The Fagus factory was a unique expression of both Bauhaus ideals: the *Gesamtkunstwerk* of the "great building" formulated in the founding manifesto of 1919, and the motto that followed after 1923: "Art and Technology – a New Unity".'[8]

The organization and internal planning, which combined manufacture and administrative offices, had already been drawn up by an experienced architect, Eduard Werner. The task for the young Walter Gropius and Adolf Meyer, commissioned by Benscheidt in the spring of 1911, was to replace Werner's exterior elevations with an image of arresting modernity, the face of a progressive company, to be clearly visible from the trains that hurried past between Hanover and the rest of Germany. Alfeld-an-der-Leine was a small provincial town, but its railway line provided a useful window to the outside world. On a more parochial level, Benscheidt was also eager to compete with Behrens, the shoe last company that he had formerly managed and which was now his competitor. The factory stood just across the tracks, inside a model of enlightened working practices but outside conventional enough, designed by Werner in 1897.

In the second phase of the Faguswerk, begun in autumn 1913, Gropius and Meyer – now in full charge – were asked to double the factory area. The emphasis was on the production hall and the expansion of the main building, which would be extended to present a suitably commanding entrance on the street side, from which most visitors approached. Their achievement was to delineate this façade strongly, marked by the emphatic brick two-storey entrance, a muscular counterpoint to the haze of glazing behind

The emphatic brick entrance to the Fagus factory, added 1913–14, serves as contrast to the apparently unsupported glazed corner and the cantilevered stair behind it.

and above it, with the staircase seen 'floating' through the glass corner.

If the Fagus factory exactly reflected the requirements of an ambitious and far-sighted industrialist, it also enabled Gropius and Meyer to use the building (unseen during the war years and extensively photographed and published only in the late 1920s) as the face of the new architecture. Photographed with editorial care and published in the right quarters, an icon of the International Style was assiduously created.

As the visitors filed through, a Who's Who of the international avant-garde from Russia, the Netherlands, France and elsewhere, and as magazine articles proliferated, Gropius put new emphasis on the use of glazing and on the structural innovation of the pier-free corners (the first of which was awkwardly engineered by means of the so-called Gropius knot, a decidedly crude junction of two iron beams at the corner). In truth, little more than a single corner of the original 1911 building actually confirmed its status,

The Fagus factory, Alfeld (1911–14), photographed in the early 1920s, with the boiler house and pebble-dashed warehouse behind the original glazed block, with its world-famous unsupported corner.

that of a glass and steel structure that had thrown away all precedent (and visible means of support), that 'seminal concept that
[had] lurked in the mind of the Modern Movement since before the
first World War'.[9] But the imagery remains impressive, while the
modern visitor is as struck by the resolution of the brickwork as
by the tentative steps towards a curtain wall. The carefully reno-
vated building is still in full working use.

The fact that Gropius discarded conventional structural support,
in the form of pier, post or column, and cantilevered the structure
out upon a steel frame, nonchalantly and transparently turning the
corner with an expanse of clear glass broken by slender glazing
bars, blinded observers to the overwhelmingly conventional
masonry structure, with its solid brick footings and recessed piers.
Images of the building to be used in any architectural discussion
were controlled by Gropius: the glazed corner was photographed
and published around the world. Few were, or even are, aware of
the large pebble-dashed warehouse, which was the most sizeable
building from the first phase. As Peter Reyner Banham argued more
than 40 years ago in *Theory and Design in the First Machine Age*,
Gropius's friendship with the historians of the Modern Movement
and the selective use of photography allowed him to overstate the
case for the pioneering importance of the Fagus building.

Banham argued for Hans Poelzig's place as the man who most
consistently worked towards 'new forms for new needs', using an
Expressionist/organic vocabulary that was developed in order to
support progressive notions of dignity in labour. These went far
beyond the limitations of the Arts and Crafts movement with the
proposal that the quality of product and work could be sustained
into a modern era with new methods.[10] In the early 1920s Behrens
himself tended to work in increasingly monumental and expressionist form, playing with colour in brickwork and even the mortars.

His corporate headquarters (1920–25) for the chemical giant Farbwerke Hoechst in Frankfurt am Main included a brilliantly stained interior, conjuring up the dyes that the company produced.

In the Deutsche Werkbund exhibition of July 1914, Gropius and Meyer had shown a model factory, the brick core of the administration block entirely housed in glazing, alongside a medium-sized single-storey work shed with a wide central nave. The unfortunate timing of the exhibition ensured that further discussion of the new architecture was long deferred, but the unbuilt designs for Fagus in the 1920s and the tantalizing but abortive collaboration between Gropius and Benscheidt Sr for a factory in the Soviet Union in 1930 point to Gropius's continued investigation of the factory as a pioneering building type, largely through the enthusiasm of a single client with exceptional vision.

More generally in the years following the First World War, there was a mismatch between the ambitions of European avant-garde architects, eager to wipe the slate clean, and post-war economic reality. The German Erich Mendelsohn had passed his wartime service as a military engineer. While on the Eastern front he filled sketchbooks with Expressionist charcoal freehand drawings which he described as railway sheds or hangars on some sheets, or factories or grain elevators on others. With their swooping lines and distinctive, hunch-shouldered mass, they supported Frank Lloyd Wright's later impression of Mendelsohn – that he was more of a modeller and sculptor than a builder and architect.

Yet Mendelsohn was optimistic for the future and as polemical as Le Corbusier in attitude. In his Berlin lecture of 1919 entitled *The Problem of a New Architecture*, he observed that 'the shifts in the mood of the age mean new challenges set by the altered building tasks of traffic, industry and culture, new possibilities for construction in the new building materials: glass – steel – concrete'.[11]

In ringing tones, he declaimed the marriage of old and new. 'Out of the posts and marble beams of the Greek temples, out of the piers and stone vaulting of the Gothic cathedral, develops the girder rhythm of the iron halls', while 'after the load-equilibrium of antiquity, after the upthrusted loads of the Middle Ages, comes the dynamic tension of reinforced concrete construction'. He spoke in a restless post-war spirit, more than ready to dust away the castellated factory gates and the old order.

Mendelsohn was also fortunate in finding steadfast clients in post-war Germany. The Luckenwalde hat factory (1921–3) in Brandenburg was his third commission for the Hermann brothers, who needed a new factory after joining forces with their competition. The expanding Steinberg Hermann company offered the young architect the opportunity to look again at his wartime sketches and think of an appropriate form for a very specific manufacturing process. There were a number of constraints. The process meant that the power house had to be central on site,

The Luckenwalde hat factory, 1921–3, architect Erich Mendelsohn. The form, strangely like his own Expressionist drawings of indeterminate structures, was driven by the need to provide huge vents above the workspace.

providing electricity for steaming the hats into shape. More importantly, noxious gases from the dyeing processes had to be removed efficiently. Turning these requirements to his advantage, Mendelsohn fashioned an abnormally steep roof, which functioned as an exhaust outlet.

Mendelsohn was concerned to present the building for publication and to point out the novel points of his design. He organized – even cropped – all photographs of the exterior to accentuate the oblique, shorn angles of the parallel sheds and the free-standing dye works. In fact, internally the reinforced concrete post-and-beam construction was not particularly novel, being made up of pre-cast angled frames, while the external treatment was in tiered and banded brick and concrete. Mendelsohn's real inventiveness was less obvious. In the spinning room he ran the power transmission shafts along hollow girders and perfected a complex system of ventilation for the upper-level drying lofts, extracting the noxious and toxic gases via a number of vents, grilles and a chimney, backed up by mechanical extractors. The novel building that resulted was quickly taken to epitomize the Expressionist approach to materials and form, in which, like Hugo Haring's lauded farm buildings and sausage factory, the function was overtly stated.

After its completion, in 1924 Mendelsohn travelled to the United States. On the *Deutschland* he met and became friendly with the architect-turned-film director Fritz Lang; each was to make good use of his early impressions. In Lang's case the result was the filmed urban fantasy *Metropolis* (1926), in which the workers and their places of work remain well below ground until they can be replaced by robots, and in Mendelsohn's, a photographic essay, *Amerika*.[12] His onward journey included Detroit and Buffalo, where he saw for himself the celebrated grain silos, the Greek temples of their moment. He described them to his wife: 'stupendous verticals of fifty to a hundred cylinders, and all this in the sharp evening light. I took photographs like mad . . . Everything else was merely a beginning.'[13]

The critic and theorist Adolf Behne rightly saw the hat factory as a mechanism in itself. From the 'expedient organization of the production process' came 'a form intended to follow and be appropriate to the functions of the business, to the production sequence, like the parts of a machine'.[14] Mendelsohn's understanding of manufacture (and, in particular, his architectural solution to the need for effective ventilation) brought him to the attention of the Leningrad Textile Trust, who in 1925 visited the Luckenwalde factory, and commissioned him to design a massive knitwear and hosiery factory, the Red Flag Factory.

The Soviet factory was for 8,000 workers and would extend a mile (1,600 metres) in length. Mendelsohn was required to design the production process, specify the machinery and to procure the

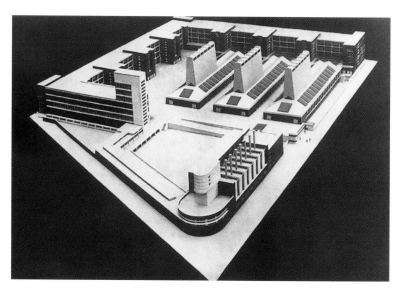

Model for the Leningrad Textile Trust 'Red Flag' factory, an impossibly ambitious commission that Mendelsohn was given in 1926 on the basis of his widely admired factory at Luckenwalde.

building materials from Germany. Despite an exemplary plan, in which three immense dye sheds (with his characteristic ventilated lofts) were wrapped on two sides by vast multi-storey factory buildings and an engine house, which with its tiered corner block recalled his Einstein Tower at Potsdam, the eventual outcome was a demoralizing failure, brought about by the use of an unskilled, badly managed labour force and inadequate materials. The exercise finally brought together the European architectural avant-garde and the Soviet social experiment.

With the introduction of the Soviet New Economic Policy (of 1921-8), the Soviet's urgent need for imported technology and expertise met the wilder shores of architectural theory. The experiment borrowed the language of the Futurists, with Soviet central planning replacing their iconoclastic romanticism. During the early years of the first Five Year Plan (1928-32), the project appeared to gather momentum. By 1930 there were some one thousand foreign architects employed in the Soviet Union engaged on numerous vast schemes of industrial and urban development, few of which achieved their immense ambitions.

Books and magazines detailing European experimental projects were eagerly imported and translated into Russian. The leading architects and their key buildings were known from the literature, from exhibitions and from their visits to Russia. When Bruno Taut moved to Moscow in 1932, he found that Soviet architects had assumed that their Western counterparts had already created the new style and enjoyed the irony that they were 'surprised to learn that there is no such architecture in Germany'.[15]

Far more ironic, however, was the fact that Soviet delegations to Detroit had long since secured the services and expertise of Albert Kahn. As the Depression took hold, a complete bureau, headed by Moritz Kahn, was set up to design and organize the building of hundreds of factories across the Soviet Union, including massive plants at Stalingrad and Cheliabinsk. In the early days, the steel was prefabricated in the USA, and virtually the entire structure, as well as tools, equipment and machinery, imported to be assembled on site. When the Kahn Soviet office was disbanded in March 1932, being unwilling to accept payment in roubles, all their design drawings and specifications were left behind, together with a growing number of Russian-trained technicians and professionals. Similarly, when Ernst May and Mart Stam were forced to leave Moscow in 1936 just before the end of the second Five Year Plan, they too were forced to hand over everything. The Soviet Union had, like the USA a century before, offered a perfect test-bed for a new version of industrialization, in which architecture and idealism would meet fleetingly on equal terms.

Unsurprisingly, Albert Kahn found little to admire in the puny efforts of his European counterparts. He had little curiosity about the Soviet experiment and a continually stated dislike of 'ultra modern' architecture. He was happy to turn his hand to heavy revivalist architecture for the mansions of his motor-manufacturing clients, Dodge and Ford, and in his view 'probably no one has done more injury than Le Corbusier and his followers'. He laid blame at the feet of writers and critics 'who too often laud their abortive attempts to the skies, form wrong public opinion and cause an era of misunderstanding' and but for them 'their sad creations would probably receive little notice'. Kahn made no claims for the modern factory building beyond it being 'sound engineering'.[16] Kahn reserved his own admiration for Peter Behrens and Auguste Perret.

Another building that was featured widely in progressive publications was the Fiat Lingotto factory in Turin, begun in 1915, in turn rooted in Kahn's work in Detroit and in Ford's introduction of efficient production systems. Giovanni Agnelli had visited Detroit and met Henry Ford, while Highland Park was published in Italy in 1915 and 1916 in the magazine *L'Industria*. The feature that marked out the engineer Giacomo Matte' Trucco's building was, however, an addition of enormous symbolic significance, the test track that looped around the rooftops of the entire factory, with a steep camber to either end. Photographs of the Fiat factory with vehicles racing overhead quickly made the factory an internationally recognized image with which the endless columns of stationary Model T Fords in Detroit could not begin to compete.

Contrary to the usual notion of a gravity-fed production process, at Fiat Lingotto a ramp spiralled up through the building, allowing the entire manufacturing cycle to occur, incrementally, until the finished vehicles emerged on the extended roof, which provided a circuit a kilometre long. In reality, Fordist efficiencies and economies were to prove far less viable in Europe, and especially in Britain where traditional craft unions and wide distrust of mechanization at all costs meant a slow and troubled introduction of moving assembly lines and standardized components. But such difficulties were of little concern to modernists in search of a model. Fiat Lingotto's apotheosis as an icon came through its publication, first by the magazine of the De Stijl group, *G*, in 1922, and then by others, in particular Le Corbusier, in *Vers une architecture*, who considered the Lingotto factory the ultimate temple to progress and speed, visibly exemplifying the aesthetic triumph of engineering.

When the young Alvar Aalto was brought in, in 1930, to consider the external details of the Toppila paper and pulp mill in Oulu, Finland, it was sheer good fortune that his friend László Moholy-Nagy should happen to pay him a visit the following summer and take a series of monumental black and white photographs which

Wood-chip container at Toppila-Vaara pulp mill, Oulu, Finland, 1930–31, the most prominent contribution to the site by architect Alvar Aalto. Commissioned by a British company, this plant closed in 1980.

played upon the mass and juxtaposition of the elements. Like huge monochrome paintings by Fernand Léger, who was, like Walter Gropius and the influential critic Sigfried Giedion, a friend of Alvar Aalto, the images burned themselves into the avant-garde architectural imagination. Philip Morton Shand completed the process by publishing the building and including it in an exhibition, thus ensuring the remote plant its iconic status.

Then, as now, an appropriate showcase in an exclusive architectural periodical ensured the uncritical admiration of the profession. In fact, Aalto had been consulted well after the main elements of the mill had been sited and designed, according to the engineering and technical requirements of the process; rather like Gropius at the Faguswerk, he was required to confine his attention to the outer shell of the building. He was given hardly more freedom when he was called in to 'design' another paper mill, Sunila, three years later. Yet Moholy-Nagy's carefully oblique angled photographs, which show the looming carapaces of the main buildings, linked by the spidery forms of the gantries and pipes (very similar to Charles Sheeler's series of photographs of River Rouge), are a celebration of the spirit of modernity and are implicitly linked to Aalto, establishing his architectural credentials in the age of the machine.

The irony was that many leading architects of the Modern Movement would simply remain with their noses pressed to the glass. European economics and politics were not conducive to major industrial expansion and certainly not to architectural risk-taking. Le Corbusier scarcely designed an industrial building in his lifetime – and then for Olivetti in 1956. Europe had no Henry Ford, Le Corbusier's hero: 'With Ford, everything is collaboration, unity of vision, unity of intentions, perfect convergence of the totality of thought and action.'

For Mies van der Rohe and others who, like him, believed that 'what Ford wants is simple and illuminating', it suggested a sort of Model T Ford production line for buildings in which the useless is progressively eliminated and the useful becomes increasingly efficient – the rational face of construction. The function of the building was, however, best expressed by its wider purpose within society. Once Mies reached the USA, he put his ideas into practice, from 1940 onwards building the svelte university campus for the Illinois Institute of Technology in Chicago. The model for the new research and development campus for industry and (later) information technology was set by Eero Saarinen's spectacular General Motors Technical Center (1950–56) at Warren, Michigan (see illustration on page 199), which pointed ahead to a post-industrial era that would have little need for either heroes or icons. Borrowing technology from the automobile industry itself, it thus moved from 'the European modernist preoccupation with the image of technology [to] a typically American concern with process'.[17]

6 Factory as Sales Tool

People like to do business with a well-dressed factory just as truly as they prefer to do business with well-dressed men.

Albert Kahn

The factory is its own most effective shop window, conveying an image of modernity or tradition, as required. The building can be an effective metaphor or it can suggest a corporate identity, intimated either by subliminal touches or by the most overt of signals.

Victorian eclectic architecture was a gift to an imaginative businessman, with a growing consumer market to reach. The Great Exhibition of 1851 showed that, to outshine the competition, manufacturers needed to resort to sheer exhibitionism. The imaginative application of exuberant ornament to factories led to a kind of commercial *architecture parlante*, arousing interest in the product and acting as a permanent free billboard.

The late eighteenth-century mill provided a functional envelope which then adapted to changes in working practice and advances in building technology. Impressive in scale, the unadorned cliffs of masonry, structural ironwork and ample glazing were efficient for their purpose, but each multi-storeyed building was largely indistinguishable from the next.

Marshalls, a long-established Leeds firm, was faced with heavy competition in a specialized area of the textile business, flax spinning. Astutely, it decided to play up the association of ancient Egypt with flax when it commissioned its latest mill around 1840.

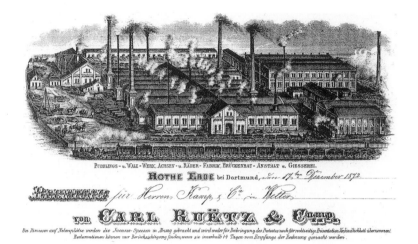

PUDDLINGS- u. WALZ- WERK, ACHSEN- u. RÄDER- FABRIK, BRÜCKENBAU- ANSTALT u. GIESSEREI.

ROTHE ERDE bei Dortmund, *den 17 ten December 1872*

Until then the Egyptian architectural revival had been confined to cemeteries and Masonic lodges.

The so-called Temple Mill, at Holbeck, was designed in 1842.[1] Not surprisingly, the street frontage of Marshalls' newest mill proved to be a highly effective promotional weapon. Egyptian dress was extended to the new warehouse and the offices, the latter an innovation in themselves, since a free-standing adminis-

The factory served as an effective promotional device on elaborately designed company letterheads.

tration block pointed to the increasing complexity of factory management.

Although the commission for the new mill was initially given to the company engineer, James Combe, he knew little of the ornamental details of Egypt, so first David Roberts, the orientalist painter, and then Joseph Bonomi the younger, an Egyptologist who had spent more than eight years in the country, were brought in to assist. Later, in 1854, Owen Jones would call on Bonomi's expertise for the design of the Egyptian Court at the Crystal Palace in Sydenham in south-east London. Bonomi was the son of the architect of the same name and the son-in-law of the painter John Martin, whose apocalyptic history paintings showing scenes such as the Fall of Babylon or Pandemonium had been, he admitted, greatly influenced by the flaming kilns and furnaces of the Black Country and Tyneside.

The splendour of Egypt for Marshalls' flax mill, 'Temple Mill', Holbeck, near Leeds, West Yorkshire, 1842, engineer James Combe.

Bonomi designed a temple-fronted office block, based on the Temple of Edfu, while the factory alongside, built in stone and punctuated by eighteen vast windows with a characteristic projecting cornice above, was based upon the Temple of Dendara. In the interest of economy, the other less visible elevations were left quite plain and were remarkable only for their great length.

Not merely canny manufacturers, the Marshalls were also famously forward-looking.[2] The choice of structure, external dress apart, was guided by a number of very practical considerations including cost and the need for overhead light, 'better and more uniform and . . . no difficulty from shadows' and its advantage for the 'arrangement of work, overlooking etc . . .'. Thus, unusually for this date, the work space was single storeyed, its vaulted ceiling allowing for generous top lighting. This was a very early example

The immense interior of Marshalls' Mill, Holbeck, designed in the 1840s and photographed prior to its demolition, the workfloor lit by many dozens of glazed cupolas.

of what became a standard factory floor design, down to the repetitive grid of columns. To optimize the use of daylight, the roof was pierced by more than 60 glazed cupolas, some 14 feet (4.27 m) in diameter, looking, according to one contemporary description, 'like cucumber frames in a garden'. Each was topped with a valve, one of a number of devices to keep temperature and humidity levels under control.[3]

Bonomi, who in later life became the curator of Sir John Soane's Museum and who, through his father, had known Soane, must have been well aware of the architect's pioneering use of top lighting – both glazed cupolas and clerestories – in his domestic work, particularly in his own house on Lincoln's Inn Fields, and in the offices at the Bank of England and at Dulwich Picture Gallery. Possibly derived from those examples, the vast shed in Leeds –

A lunar landscape, the glazed cupolas above the workfloor at Marshalls' 'Temple' Mill, Holbeck. Originally the roof was grassed over and mown by sheep, until one fell through a rooflight.

demolished in the 1960s (the Egyptian offices survive) – had a reasonable claim to be the first top-lit industrial shed in the world.

Linen mills required stable temperatures, and this was achieved by insulating the roof with earth, to a depth of eight inches (20.32 cm). Seeded with grass, the meadow was kept neatly mown by sheep until an unfortunate incident, in which an animal fell to its doom on the machinery below, demonstrated the drawbacks of a rooftop pasture punctuated with skylights. Other matters were better considered: the turf undulated, enabling the run-off water to flow down into the hollow cast-iron columns below. The steam engines that powered the drive shafts were housed in the brick-vaulted basement and provided the heating that gave the necessary levels of warmth and humidity for the process. Inevitably, the original factory chimney at 'Temple' Mill was an Egyptian obelisk. After cracking in 1852, it was replaced by a more conventional, and no doubt more practical, chimney.

Nor was the Egyptian theme confined to the exterior. Bonomi delighted in the decorative potential of the style. On the factory floor, the iron columns were topped by palm- and papyrus-leaf capitals, while the beam engine was ornamented by appropriately Egyptian pylons and a regulator in the form of a winged solar disc.[4] A model of this engine was displayed at the Great Exhibition of 1851, another effective forum for publicity for manufacturers among both their peers and the public.

The mill even found its place in fiction, and John Marshall was generally considered to be one of the models for the composite figure of Mr Trafford in Disraeli's *Sybil* (1845). The writer was fascinated by the novel arrangements, noting that the mill was

one of the marvels of the district; one might almost say of the country: a single room, spreading over nearly two acres, and holding more than two thousand workpeople. The roof of groined arches, lighted by ventilating domes at the height of eighteen feet, was supported by hollow cast-iron columns, through which the drainage of the roof was effected.

He compared the usual low-ceilinged workrooms in storeyed factories. 'At Mr Trafford's, by an ingenious process, not unlike that which is practised in the House of Commons, the ventilation was also carried on from below, so that the whole building was kept at a steady temperature, and little susceptible to atmospheric influences.' The arrangement, Disraeli added, benefited the workforce and gave ease of movement, cut down accidents and permitted 'superior inspection and general observation'.[5]

The unique features of the mill meant that it quickly became well known, through admiring reports in the professional and technical journals. Such magazines provided useful and detailed information on the design, technology and operation of new factories, as well as listing hundreds of newly patented devices in every issue. The exchange of ideas and experience between manufacturers took place largely on paper.

For those with more conventional premises, the huge industrial chimney stack was the nineteenth-century equivalent to a neon sign or flamboyant logo. In the freewheeling spirit of Victorian eclecticism, Robert Rawlinson's book, *Boiler and Factory Chimneys* (1877), discussed the architectural possibilities. However dour the mill or factory, it could still flaunt itself with a soaring columnar chimney, detailed according to an array of historical styles, the elaboration usually reaching a crescendo at the very top. Patterned or polychrome brick, terracotta or ceramic panels, battlements and lavish ornament brought much needed colour to the monochrome scenery of

Victorian textile towns. There was a continual race to erect a yet taller chimney. For a time the record was held by a Manchester printing works, Schwabe's, whose chimney soared to 321 feet (97.8 m) – well above the heads of all its competitors, the Petronas Towers of its day.

Late nineteenth-century businesses enjoyed establishing a link between their buildings and their products. Doulton marketed their goods very overtly: their Lambeth factory was encrusted with ceramics. Similarly there was an inescapable commercial logic in dressing Templeton's Glasgow carpet factory in the glowing colours, textures and motifs of a Byzantine Gothic palace, from the pages of John Ruskin's *Stones of Venice* (1851–3). William Leiper's exuberant design, built in 1889 overlooking Glasgow Green, in which colour and pattern are marshalled to powerful effect, sits well in Glasgow alongside neighbours in the Greek, Italian Renaissance and Gothic styles.

The design of Templeton's factory is unambiguously based upon

An appropriately modelled pottery tympanum in terracotta by George Tinworth for Doulton's Works, Lambeth, London, 1878, architect R. Stark Wilkinson.

that of an oriental carpet. The theme is played out energetically in a frieze of multicoloured faience set into an Italian Renaissance zig-zagging *bargello* pattern surmounted by a defensive-looking cresting of brick machicolations. In the centre of the main elevation is an upper-level loggia, and corbelled turrets rhythmically mark out the full width. According to Leiper's architectural partner, the decision to pursue the Byzantine style came from the clients, who 'as patrons of the arts, resolved not alone in the interests of the workers, but also of the citizens, to erect instead of the ordinary and common factory something of permanent architectural interest and beauty'.[6]

The visibility of the building was, no doubt, a prompt to the

Eclectic and eyecatching architecture ensured notice for Templeton's Glasgow carpet factory and its products.

comfortable classes of Glasgow, contemplating the purchase of Turkish-patterned carpets for their new suburban houses.

An impressive image of a factory, usually in the form of a somewhat idealized bird's-eye view of the works, often headed company stationery, packaging and advertising material, acting as a cost-effective form of publicity before widespread commercial advertising. Breweries made sure that their buildings decorated the labels of their bottles; Carlsberg's gate supported by elephants at their main Copenhagen plant was unforgettable. Carreras cigar boxes were decorated with the Baroque swirls and curlicues of the Seville royal factory, a point underlined by the fact that it was the setting for Bizet's popular opera of the 1870s, *Carmen*. In Dresden, the Yenidze cigarette factory of 1907 was built to look like a mosque, with minarets and dome, a strong message about the oriental exoticism of tobacco. 'Day and night, during profitable and unprofitable business hours, this building is an advertisement for the owner, at no cost to the publicity account.'[7]

The ornamented pediment of the administration block of Argyll Motors at Alexandria, near Glasgow, similarly made the point. A carved Argyll car bursts through the stonework, accompanied by goddesses of speed with their robes caught in the slipstream and by handsomely idealized workers bearing the attributes of their trade, such as an anvil and gear wheel. The automobile was, for a few years, an expensive (often unreliable) handcrafted item, a fact that was reflected in an architectural approach more fit for a bank than a factory.

Charles Halley, a local architect, built the 760-foot-long (231.6 m) administration block in the Baroque Revival style, a luxurious, well-crafted building to match the vehicles. The local red sandstone is banded and rusticated, with balustrades and a gigantic

ornamented central tower, offering a reassuring sense of enduring qualities, well suited to the expensive end of automobile manufacture. Inside, the managing director presided from Georgian-style offices, while an Elizabethan Revival boardroom was provided for the directors.[8] Each worker had a numbered washbasin of his own. For the company, 'The few extra hundreds required to provide a motor factory second to none in the world have been repaid already and with interest, by the very advertisement that such a building is in itself.'

At the opposite extreme was Carl Benscheidt who, when he built the Fagus factory in 1911 to manufacture wooden shoe-lasts, was eager to use progressive design to flag up the new technology and progressive nature of his American-funded business. As we

A vehicle bursts through the pediment, accompanied by figures with appropriate attributes. The Argyll Motors car factory, Alexandria, near Glasgow, 1905–6, architect Charles Halley.

have seen, Adolf Meyer and Walter Gropius provided an image of transparency and structural daring for an expanding business. Clearly visible from the busy railway line that ran through the small town of Alfeld in lower Saxony, people could immediately grasp from the unfamiliar architecture, the clean lines and modern materials that this was no traditional factory. By implication, the business was highly innovative, while the accuracy and quality of the product were implicit in the sharp, precise forms. Shortly after the first phase had been completed, an admiring article was published in *Der Industriebau*, emphasizing the revolutionary aspects of the building. Benscheidt ordered 1,500 offprints of the article, to distribute to clients. He knew that 'an exemplary building could also be an excellent advertisement'.

Publicity was also generated by first-hand knowledge. In the nineteenth century it had become commonplace to offer tours of works to interested visitors, just as their grandparents might have taken in a trip to Coalbrookdale or the Soho Manufactory on a Picturesque journey towards the Wye Valley or North Wales. Factory visits offered an opportunity to interest potential employees as well as to sound out markets. High above the Van Nelle factory in Rotterdam, customers could try the company's coffee, tea and cocoa in a glass-walled, cantilevered tearoom, or survey the city skyline from a nautical-styled observation terrace above, while visitors were always made welcome at Spirella's 'Castle Corset' in Letchworth Garden City. Even today, the Avent factory (2000) for baby products in rural Suffolk encourages local health visitors to visit the works, where they can wonder at the million-pound injection moulding machines that press four vacuum-packed bottles out of silicon grains every twelve seconds. Seven of these machines cost almost twice as much as the smart new building by Fletcher Priest Architects, a portal frame clad with sinuous profiled steel panels and full-height glazing, through which passers-by can see the machines toiling futuristically. As a replacement for the huddle of 1930s and '70s sheds and warehouses that stood on the site, Avent considers its new factory to be the best possible asset, for publicity as for everything else.[9]

The car manufacturer Citroën made the most of its location in east-central Paris, where the Javel plant occupied a huge swathe of the left bank of the Seine, just down-river from the Eiffel Tower. In the late 1920s there was no escaping Citroën's pre-eminence as the major French motor manufacturer. André Citroën had started with a daily production of thirty 10cv vehicles in 1919, but just eight years later the daily output had risen to four hundred.[10]

The public was invited to visit the factory and a book was produced to celebrate the factories and their breathtaking scale, covering some 77 hectares by 1929. The employees enjoyed a progressive regime that provided them with benefits from calisthenics to crèches.

The model for the manufacturing system had, inevitably, come from the USA, where senior executives from Citroën, with their counterparts from Benz, Renault and Fiat among others, had gone to investigate the methods of Taylor and Ford and, on return, had introduced their own assembly-line systems, emulating Michigan. André Citroën was quick to realize the advantages of a strong corporate identity and brought his flair to the design of the dealerships and service centres, all smartly and distinctively styled. Citroën's factories and garages built up a strong corporate image, much as did Bata's elegant city stores in their easily recognizable Modern Movement company livery.

Citroën's cars were for sale to the widest possible public, being lightweight and cheap. The market for motor cars was potentially limitless, if still untried in Europe, and the sophisticated Citroën publicity machine took maximum advantage of stylish events such as the Exposition des Arts Décoratifs of 1925 and epoch-making moments such as Charles Lindbergh's crossing of the Atlantic in 1927. These culminated in Citroën's own epic international motor safaris, beginning with the Saharan Croisière Noire (1925), then one to the South Pole in 1927 and in 1931 from Beirut to Beijing.

Ford, too, was highly alert to the possibilities of publicity for its world-beating enterprise. The most impressive product the company had to sell was Henry Ford himself, and his thoughts, dreams and achievements, with which came his unpalatable views on race and society. Despite this, Mr Ford proved endlessly marketable. The Ford company dealt only in a relentless roll-call of records and superlatives. In 1913 a newsreel showed the new moving production line at Highland Park in action (the first in the world) and 12,000 of the workforce posed for a group photograph (the largest ever), a companion shot to that showing the day's production of Model Ts. Tens of thousands of visitors came each year to see the plants, first to Highland Park (the largest automobile plant in the world) and then to the integrated plant at River Rouge, which by 1929 employed 103,000 workers on a site unrivalled anywhere in the world except for the Krupp works at Essen in Germany.

At the Rouge plant metaphor was piled upon metaphor: 'each unit . . . a carefully designed gear which meshes with other gears and operated in synchronism with them, the whole forming one huge, perfectly-timed, smoothly operating industrial machine of almost unbelievable efficiency.'[11] In 1927 Charles Sheeler was commissioned to photograph the plant, and the resulting images, reinforced by the powerful murals that the company president Edsel Ford commissioned from Diego Rivera for the Detroit Institute of Arts, showed the potential of a mechanistic figurative vocabulary. Frida Kahlo, Rivera's wife, painted her self-portrait in 1932, and set herself against two monolithic landscapes, one her native Mexico, one Ford's and Kahn's River Rouge. In a demure white muslin dress but with a cigarette in hand, she straddles the two worlds that a modern, independent woman of the time confronted.[12]

Very early at the Faguswerk, the Benscheidts had used photography for various purposes. From the beginning, they commissioned construction shots of the building, partly to keep their American financial partners informed of progress. Edmund Lill, who was selected by Gropius for the job, photographed the buildings in 1912 and then, after their long delayed completion, again in 1922. Another photographer, Albert Renger-Patzsch (also blessed by Gropius), took a further series in 1928 which included both the products and the industrial process, machines and unusual but selective details of the buildings. Nothing that detracted from the notion of 'form following function and construction' was included. These images were widely used in the company's international advertising campaigns, as well as in the architect's energetic campaign to present the building as the first structure of the 'new architecture', as it was epitomized in the catalogue to Gropius's Berlin exhibition of 1930.[13]

Such industrial commissions, as well as being an enduring and powerful form of public relations exercise, pointed to the notion of business patronage of the arts and, from it, the rewards of corporate sponsorship.

If the factory might serve as a sales vehicle, so too could the model village. Henry Ford's Greenfield Village at Dearborn was an architectural cabinet of curiosities, heritage bits and pieces collected from everywhere and designed for the publicity purposes of the company. Centre stage were shrines to the industrial past in the shape of reconstructed workshops of heroes such as Thomas Edison and Ford himself.

Lord Leverhulme's Port Sunlight was an industrial village but, bearing the name of his soap bar, it also offered an excellent publicity vehicle. The widely publicized philanthropic efforts of its founder, together with the charming name and obvious image of domestic cleanliness, were no doubt a considerable factor in the buoyant sales that the company quickly established in the early 1900s. In cul-de-sac after cul-de-sac of traditional-style cottages with all modern conveniences, the squeaky-clean windows, freshly laundered nets and well-scrubbed doorsteps were clear evidence of the effective use of foaming Sunlight suds. The daily lives of Lord Leverhulme's workforce and their families were a constant advertisement for the efficacy of his products.

In the inter-war period, the London Brick Company in Bedfordshire made their self-evident point with a brick-built garden village, overshadowed by clusters of factory chimneys emblazoned with the company acronym. Crittalls, manufacturers of the eponymous metal windows, seized a similar advantage when they built their factory at Silver End near Witham in Essex and developed a model industrial village around it. All the houses, whether polite neo-Georgian brick cottages or improbable Modern Movement houses, flat-roofed, rendered and whitewashed, bravely bright against the repetitive Essex landscape, were fitted with the windows that came out of the factory gates a few metres away. At Kirk Sandall in South Yorkshire, a garden village built for employees of the Pilkington glass company, the hotel, designed in 1934, celebrated the firm's latest acquisition, Vitrolite, an American company making glass-cladding material. Bands of black, shell-pink, pearl and turquoise celebrated its decorative potential on the exterior, while indoors the theme continued: now in subtle blues, greens and ivory with black and green pressed-glass floor tiles underfoot.[14]

Chimneys emblazoned with the initials of the London Brick Company overshadow the company village at Stewartby, Bedfordshire. Architect E. Vincent Harris, 1927 onwards.

Semi-detached workers' cottages with steel windows, factory village for Crittalls windows manufacture. Silver End, near Witham, Essex, architect Sir Thomas Tait, 1926–32.

Fort Dunlop, manufacturing motor tyres, ensured that it caught the eye of every driver heading to Birmingham past its brick industrial castle. During the First World War, funding was secured and planning began for a new system of arterial roads around London. Then as now, alterations to major roads heralded a development opportunity, and in west Middlesex the opportunity opened for a huge industrial expansion, much of which, though changed in function and appearance, remains.

In wartime, the rapid building of dozens of new munitions factories had revolutionized notions of the possible: concrete, steel and electricity had come of age. In 1916 Thomas Wallis, who had begun the war in the Office of Works, set up the architectural practice of Wallis, Gilbert & Partners (there was never a Gilbert) in collaboration with Truscon, combining the advantages of in-house engineering expertise and the freedom to advertise and seek out

A manager's detached house, Silver End, with a full range of Crittall windows.

new clients – commercial activities forbidden to the architectural profession.[15]

For ten years the practice worked closely with Truscon, building major factories such as the General Electric Co. Ltd, on Electric Avenue at Witton outside Birmingham (fronted by an Egyptian-detailed administration building), and the Wrigley Products factory of 1926 in North Wembley, where mushroom columns and slabs replaced a post-and-beam structure.

The rebuilding of the post-war economy in the late 1920s was a boon to those American companies looking for a break into the European market for consumer goods. Britain was their bridgehead and allowed them to get round the Tariff Act of 1927. The new arterial roads offered ease of distribution; planning controls were scant on the adjacent greenfield sites; and the increased flexibility offered by a now-reliable electricity supply meant that factories had virtual freedom of location. Unchecked suburban expansion also meant that a new workforce was at hand.

In the late 1920s factory-boom companies streamed into areas to the north-west and west of London such as Wembley, Park Royal, Ealing and Perivale. Freed from backstreet obscur-ity, in the case of an existing company such as Smith's Potato Crisps in Cricklewood, they were now ideally sited to catch the eye of thousands of potential customers as the droves of passing motorists took the Great West Road and other main routes in or out of town. An entirely new range of products for kitchen, home and garage appeared in front of an increasingly affluent public.

Most companies built their administrative headquarters alongside factories, an American practice. The architectural choice was generally the Moderne style, concrete-rendered and painted white, colourfully ornamented with Art-Deco-derived trim. The

area became a 'roadside gallery of modern architecture'.[16] Thomas Wallis's 'Fancy' factories attracted a great deal of critical opprobrium from his professional peers, but pleased the public with their colourful façades designed to look more like cinemas than factories. Jostling on the kerbsides were dozens of exuberant frontages, but those of Firestone and Hoover – both designed by Wallis, Gilbert & Partners – particularly caught the spirit of the Jazz Age.

The Firestone factory was an American commission. When Harvey Firestone built his works at Akron, Ohio, in 1910 – to cope with the huge orders required by the Ford Motor Company – he mapped out the manufacturing process with a model and a piece of string. Seventeen years later Firestone decided to build a manu-

The Art Deco Hoover factory, built to attract the eye of passing motorists on Western Avenue in west London. Now converted to corporate headquarters and supermarket. 1932–5, architects Wallis, Gilbert & Partners.

facturing and distribution plant in Britain and turned to Thomas Wallis. For publicity purposes the speed of the building operation, despite its efficiency, was greatly exaggerated.

The gleaming white Firestone administration block stood back and above the level of the road, the stage for a building that, with its columned façade and its brilliantly coloured ceramic ornament in the Egyptian style, had a powerful theatrical presence. The faience details were the first to be picked off by the wrecker's ball as demolition began on August Bank Holiday Monday in 1980.

Behind the administration building stretched a series of linked blocks: first a classic single-storeyed Kahn-type factory with generous fenestration and north lights, then behind it a four-storey block for departments dealing with the receipt and despatch of goods. At the extremity of the sequence was the power house, picking up the ornament of the front elevation. The floors and

The demolition (August 1980) of the administration block of the Firestone Tyre & Rubber Company factory, the handsomest of Wallis, Gilbert & Partners' Art Deco factories on the Great West Road, London.

foundations were of reinforced concrete, the frame of steel, clad in concrete with brick and glass panels.

Thomas Wallis considered that colour had a beneficial effect on the workers and that they would take pride in the fact that their place of work was a recognizable landmark. He was also fully aware of the advertising potential, the wisdom of 'a little money spent on something to focus the attention of the public', which would 'give proportionately better results than that obtained from the large yearly expenditure so often incurred in usual advertising'.[17]

In their house journal, Curry's, manufacturers of cycles and radios, trumpeted the 'incalculable' publicity value of their location on the Great West Road, 'which will advertise Curry's to the world'. Like many of their neighbours, Curry's floodlit the roadside elevation and tower of their building in exuberant fashion. So too did Hoover, from 1932 onwards Wallis, Gilbert & Partners' latest clients, with a site on Western Avenue. The most exuberant of the nine 'fancy' factories, its colourful eclectic façade appeared on all kinds of promotional items for the company, while from the rear no railway passenger could miss the neon-lit legend 'Hoover beats as it sweeps as it cleans'. The heavily faceted and ornamental elevation of the Hoover building, like that of the Firestone factory, might have been designed expressly to be lit up by night. Like Mendelsohn's Petersdorff department store in Breslau of 1928, which emphasized the effects with external strip lighting and white curtaining, illumination and shadow dramatized the forms of the Hoover building, giving local people and passers-by a continuous show, the twentieth-century version of the blazing banks of windows in the early gas-lit mills.

Eventually the riot of exhibitionist architecture became, like the exhibits at the Great Exhibition, self-defeating. In the later 1930s

A return to brick and sobriety; the Gillette factory, Great West Road, London, 1930s, architect Banister Fletcher.

The Great Workroom at the Johnson Wax factory, Racine, Wisconsin. Light enters above the dendriform capitals in a luminous building designed to celebrate the virtues of polish. 1936–9, architect Frank Lloyd Wright.

Gillette and Guinness Breweries, both located in the same area of west London, decided upon a more sober approach, using plain English brick and employing, respectively, two respected architects, Banister Fletcher and Giles Gilbert Scott, who proved adept at paring down Classical and ornamental elements to the minimum in their stately additions to the industrial landscape.

Streamlined modernity was a great antidote to the Depression. Architecturally, it seemed confident and progressive, or, in Frank Lloyd Wright's ringing phrase, 'sure of itself and clean for its purpose, clean as a hound's tooth'. At his Johnson Wax administration building at Racine, Wisconsin, horizontality – brickwork with strands of crystal tubing laid through it at intervals and as clerestory lighting – gave a suitably shiny, glittery image to the headquarters of a polishing empire which 'became a different company the day the building opened. We achieved international attention because that building represented and symbolized the quality of everything we did in terms of products, people, the working environment . . . '.[18] Inside, the spectacular Great Workroom was supported upon dendriform columns, a mere 9 inches (22.86 cm) in diameter at their base, spreading to a 20-foot (6.09 m) fan upon the roof, with light pouring down around the edges. After the war, Wright added the even sleeker Research Tower, in which broader bands of glass tubes dominated narrower strips of brickwork, forming, as the architect saw it, a torch to illuminate the business around the world. Such potent images were well served by the contemporary growth of photojournalism. Johnson Wax could not have bought the newspaper and magazine publicity that their building gave them for 'two or more millions of dollars', as Wright put it.[19] In downtown Los Angeles, the Coca-Cola bottling plant assumed the guise of a great ocean liner, complete with port-holes and upper deck. Each corner was marked by a huge, instantly recognizable

A huge bottle helps to identify the Coca-Cola Bottling Plant, Los Angeles, 1936–7, architect Robert V. Derrah.

bottle, expressing the unquenchable optimism of the makers of America's favourite beverage.

The modern business, its product exhaustively advertised in the media, is less excited about such exposure, but contemporary imagery still retains a strong pull, despite its tendency to date and suggest the fashions of yesterday. Foster Associates' Renault Distribution centre of 1983 outside Swindon, more warehouse than factory, quickly became the stylish backdrop to many of their advertising campaigns – its cabling and pierced metal web acting out the form of a tent. Design-led companies are, obviously, much concerned with the architecture of their factories and, on occasion, prove faithful clients to their architects. In 1976 the leading furniture makers Herman Miller had commissioned an elegantly clad

The Los Angeles Coca-Cola Bottling Plant was designed to emulate a great ocean-going liner, with its decks, port-holes and other nautical features. The marketing potential of such a building was an enormous asset.

shed from Nicholas Grimshaw in Bath and, a few years later, a distribution centre based on the same structural system, but with different cladding, at Chippenham in Wiltshire.

Another furniture company, Vitra, near Basle in Switzerland, also commissioned a steel-clad shed from Grimshaw and then surrounded it by an entire menagerie of 'signature' buildings. Like a variant on Henry Ford's collection of old buildings shipped into Greenfield from the Cotswolds and other places equally far away, the collection includes a 'fire station' by Zaha Hadid, a 'factory' by Frank Gehry and a conference centre by Tadao Ando. Now Ando has designed a new Benetton factory at Treviso in northern Italy. The name of an internationally known architect generates useful column inches in design-conscious publications and, as ever, free advertising.

Aiming at a less elite audience, functional forms, such as the masts and tension cables that usefully support wide-span roofs

The use of colour, exposed Meccano-like elements and the very visible masts ensured that Foster & Partners' 1983 Renault Distribution Centre at Swindon, Wiltshire, became a useful tool within Renault's advertising strategy.

The Vitra 'factory' near Basle, Switzerland, was never likely to become a workplace. However, Vitra as a furniture-design company benefited from the attention given to Frank Gehry's 1987 building and its companions in what has become a museum of architecture.

The undulating roof structure of Valode & Pistre's L'Oréal cosmetics factory, Aulnay-sous-Bois, France, of 1988–91 floats above its setting in an unprepossessing industrial suburb, ensuring that it is as prominent from the air as from the ground.

With their Funder factory at St Veit, of 1988–9, the Austrian practice Coop Himmelblau has demonstrated that a boardworks can be as eyecatching as a contemporary art museum.

and efficiently create uninterrupted interior space, are also effective eye-catchers. With sites prominent in the landscape or along a motorway, even from the air, leading European firms such as Benetton (Treviso), l'Oreal (Aulnay-sous-Bois), and Igus (Cologne) have all benefited from their visibility – challenging the anonymity of the sleek shed.

The Igus factory (1992) is for a company making injection-moulded plastics and embodies all the most progressive ideas towards flexibility, modern working practice and tradition (the last consisting of natural top lighting and ventilation through domes – invoking the shades of Marshalls Mill in Leeds). Nicholas Grimshaw, chosen as architect on the basis of his track record with panelled industrial buildings over the previous two decades, defended the two ostentatious yellow masts that tower above the slick metal shed: 'I make no apology for [their] powerful impact . . . I believe they give the project a great image and excitement'.[20] The engineers, Whitby & Bird, might prefer to emphasize the real innovations, the demountable office 'pods' and other portable elements that are buried deep and unseen within the clear span, airport-terminal-sized shed.

For more self-effacing times, the factory built in Malmesbury, Wiltshire, in the late 1990s by Chris Wilkinson Architects for Dyson's revolutionary vacuum cleaner and washing machine plant has a quieter profile, with a pacific, undulating roofline rippling through the landscape. Hardly had it opened, than much of the production was forced to move to the Far East because of labour costs.

Yet, in a move that bucks every current trend, in the New Year of 2002 the car manufacturers Volkswagen moved into their just-completed crystal palace, the Glaeserne Manufaktur, set in parkland in the centre of Dresden. In a sparkling vehicle

assembly plant, designed by Henn architects, the newest model VW (the Phaeton) is put together from parts brought in by freight-train from factories elsewhere, and the finished product is then displayed in a twelve-storey glass tower to full public gaze.[21] For once, the manufacturing process is back in sight and industry is right at the centre of the city: James Watt would surely approve.

The Dyson vacuum cleaner factory, Malmesbury, Wiltshire, completed in 1999, architect Chris Wilkinson. A brave stab at retaining manufacture in Britain, despite which, much of the production now takes place in the Far East.

The Volkswagen 'Transparent Factory' near Dresden, 1999–2001. Clean manufacture returns to the city in the 21st century. Architect and engineer, Henn Architects.

7 Factory as Laboratory or Laboratory as Factory?

Factories should look like what they are – factories and nothing else.
Moritz Kahn

The lifespan of any particular industry has never been predictable and the vicissitudes of politics, products and people add to the air of uncertainty. A brief snapshot of one company, extending over more than 200 years of its history, illustrates the point.

In 1785 John Hall, an apprentice millwright, arrived in Dartford, Kent, and set up in a shack as a self-employed smith. Soon becoming a sought-after and busy mechanic for the various mills that processed corn, paper, oil and gunpowder, as well as for local people and businesses, he soon had to move to larger premises. Around him, his former apprentices and erstwhile business partners formed a network of men continuously pushing at the limits of mechanization and looking out for patents to buy, from home and abroad. They interested themselves in paper-making and canning machinery as well as rotary printing, signalling a tempting world of commercial possibilities through innovative manufacture.

John Hall, a careful man who could see the risks involved in the unknown and untried, concentrated on the field with which he was most familiar, heavy engineering. An early nineteenth-century letterhead for the Dartford Ironworks described John Hall & Sons as 'Engineers, Steam Engine Manufacturers and Millwrights, Iron and Brass Founders' and proudly listed their products, which included 'machinery for plate glass works, roll bars and plates for paper

R. A. Lister & Co., Victorian mechanized disorder. Tricycle factory, Dursley, Gloucestershire, 1880s.

R. A. Lister & Co. workers using machinery powered by overhead shafts. Tricycle factory, Dursley, c. 1890.

engines, hydraulic and screw presses, diving bells, pumps, cranes etc.' The powerful beam engines for which the company became best known went down the Thames estuary to every corner of Britain and around the world.

After Hall's death in 1836 the company continued under his sons, trading as J. (John) & E. (Edward) Hall. By the time that Edward died in the 1870s, the firm had become a classic case of a second-generation family enterprise burdened with inadequate, old-fashioned buildings, out-of-date plant, an unchanged catalogue of goods and a shrinking workforce. Fortunately for its survival, the firm's main customers, the local cement and paper manufacturers, had remained faithful.

The arrival in 1878 of Everard Hesketh, a young engineer who had intended to spend only a few months with the company, transformed the future prospects of J. & E. Hall. When visiting the Great International Exhibition in Paris that year, he chanced upon Paul Giffard's cold-air machine and decided to test it. Impressed by its potential, he took out patents on a number of improvements to the original machine. J. & E. Hall developed and then manufactured their own variant. The gamble paid off, for Hesketh had seen the enormous potential in marine refrigeration and dockside cold storage, and he speedily switched from the cold-air machine to the far more efficient CO_2 system, transforming the market.

As befitted a firm run by engineers, new technology posed no fears: since 1882 the factory had been lit by electricity. In November 1900 J. & E. Hall became a public company, 'to establish, conduct and carry on ice works, ice stores, meat freezing and chiller establishments', a field in which they had become world leaders. In 1906 they diversified into commercial vehicle production, on an adjacent site, making lorries and buses under the name of Hallford, which flourished with wartime contracts but failed thereafter.

The company then moved, with greater success, into the manufacture of lifts and escalators, always remaining on John Hall's original Dartford site of 1785. As a child living in the East Anglian countryside in the 1950s, the mysterious doings of J. & E. Hall were a continual topic of conversation at home: both my maternal grandfather and his brother-in-law, my great-uncle, were marine engineers and were employed by the company for all of their working lives, my grandfather steering the company through the Depression years. In the 1970s the flourishing business rebuilt its factory and merged with an aluminium company, as a result being renamed APV Hall Products Ltd.

The bicentenary year, 1985, was marked with a book and appropriate celebrations, despite the telltale trickle of redundancies which had begun in the early 1980s.[1] When change came, it was with the speed of an avalanche: in 1987 the company negotiated the sale of their valuable town centre site to the B&Q home improvement superstore group, and by 1990 the factory had been demolished, its site to become just another retail park. In 1995 the name of J. & E. Hall was resurrected under the ownership of the McQuay Group, an American air conditioning company, itself owned by a Malaysian banking conglomerate.

At the time of writing, a remnant of the company still operates under this name from an office in Dartford, overseeing a handful of depots scattered around the country. Desperately reduced from a proud history of manufacture and innovation, its business is now servicing air conditioning and refrigeration units made by others, elsewhere. For shareholders in the parent company, watching the financial indices far away in Asia, the historic name and history of J. & E. Hall Ltd means nothing, and the fate of its modern successor of little consequence. This familiar enough story shows how deadly have been the recent divisions between finance, industry and society.

Factories have become far removed from everyday experience. Assembly-line production is familiar only from television coverage of factory closures or sitcoms, films and advertisements. Dagenham and Cowley, suburbs of London and Oxford respectively, might as well be in Taiwan. Even Renault's proud new 150-hectare campus, the Technocentre, inaugurated in its centenary year of 1998, is hidden away in the featureless countryside near Saint-Quentin-en-Yvelines, a new town to the west of Paris. Few companies welcome interested visitors, industrial processes are arcane rituals to most people, while health and safety considerations conspire to prohibit public access to the factory floor.

Manufacturing is largely invisible, but not as charmingly camouflaged as the wartime Douglas aircraft plant in Santa Monica in California, which concealed its rooftop from the enemy as an imitation suburban street. Most modern factories or 'labour warehouses', the latter dedicated to assembling components made by more highly skilled workers somewhere else, are geographically remote from the consumer. Factories or tax-free assembly zones in the poorest countries of Central and South America and Asia emulate the worst conditions to be found in Victorian mills and come to our notice only when, because of their locked safety exits, a fire claims the lives of those within. The garment workers of Thailand or Taiwan, filling the racks in malls across the developed world; the toy makers of mainland China, turning out the cracker fillers and party bags for Western festivals and celebrations; and the car workers of Mexico and Eastern Europe, ensuring mobility for commuters in the main financial centres, are thousands of kilometres away from the markets they supply – just as, increasingly, are the call centres that field the consumers' calls for help or complaint.

Naomi Klein wrote her angry book *No Logo* in a disused factory in the former garment district of Toronto. While on a research trip, she visited a Jakarta textiles factory where the women were making raincoats, and discovered that the label that they were supplying, *London Fog*, was the one that had been manufactured in her Toronto block, even in her own apartment.[2]

The factory, with its emphasis on the repetitive and organized processes of manufacture, in the dictionary definition of 'a building, or buildings, with plant for the manufacture of goods', has altered beyond recognition. The state-of-the-art factory in its campus or landscaped Science or Business Park, close to a motorway intersection or university, is more likely to be concerned with research and development than assembly or manufacture, in a setting as green and attractive as money spent on careful planting and a budget for high quality maintenance can make it. While Frank Lloyd Wright's office and research headquarters for Johnson at Racine, Wisconsin, emphatically turned inwards, to ignore the unpleasant surroundings, many modern locations have been chosen for their landscape – a reaction to an atavastic memory of the Victorian mill town or the inter-war trading estate.

The setting of the landed estate is as congenial to the biotech industry as it was to the *manufactures royales*, an image of reassuring and established order in the face of the unknown. Mature eighteenth-century parkland, oaks, lawn and a generous lake provide the impeccable surroundings of the campus outside Cambridge where the Human Genome Project has its home. The administration lords it in a restored Georgian mansion, the stables and outbuildings provide conference and meeting areas and the research laboratories and staff facilities nestle in a series of carefully staggered blocks, pristine in their uniform of burnished metal and glass, at the other side of the park. The world of work here is as closed and obscure as the world of manufacture or academe.

Viewed from outside, these enclosed and luxurious monolithic complexes, in Britain in pleasant surroundings often tucked into the protected landscape of the Green Belt, have become the working equivalent of the upmarket shopping mall or the gated residential complex – highly privileged environments for the car-borne that remain entirely secure and separate from the outside world. The certainty that their activities will eventually impinge upon us all, in unspecified ways, merely compounds their unsettling nature, architecturally impeccably well-mannered, entirely multinational and utterly uncommunicative.

In Douglas Coupland's novel *Microserfs* (1995), the scene is set on the Microsoft campus in Seattle, where trees and black-windowed buildings 'seemingly clicked into place with a mouse' dot the

Parkland landscape and an 18th-century mansion provide the setting for the Sanger Centre, the base for the Human Genome Project at Hinxton outside Cambridge, England, 1995–7, architect Sheppard Robson.

continuously mown lawns. It shifts to Silicon Valley in California, where the same eery, clean landscape is repeated: slick buildings surrounded by immaculately groomed grass, looking like smart Japanese audio equipment, 'machine-shaped' to express the arcane and inscrutable processes within.

Unusually for the USA, where most new automobile plants are in the Southern states, if not beyond the national boundary, the new Cadillac works, Jefferson North, have remained close to their roots in Michigan. Designed by Albert Kahn Inc., who remain the premier architectural firm in the field, they cope with their setting by design. Physically buffered from the nearby residential areas by a sequence of green spaces, five-lane service roads and then 20-foot (6.09 m) high 'berms' or mounds, 'the design of the Jefferson plant explains the changing relationship between the community and industry, enforced by the principle of globalization, the dominant feature to the economy of capitalisation. The result is physical dissociation between the site-specific community and the site-less economy'.[3]

But equally the modern factory has an affinity with the Picturesque. In rural locations, the constraints of landscape can dictate the form of the architecture. David Mellor's cutlery factory, sited in an Area of Outstanding Natural Beauty north of Sheffield, was designed by Michael Hopkins in close consultation with his industrial designer client. The conical, lead roofed building settles tactfully into the 'footprint' of a gasholder formerly on the site and, surrounded by trees, makes a quiet neighbour to the stone cottages and farmhouses of the valley. The siting of the new Ercol furniture factory, a sliver of a building elegantly set amidst the Buckinghamshire woods, benefits employees, company image and the local economy.[4] In another wood near Mulhouse in France, the polycarbon panels used as cladding by Jacques Herzog and Pierre de Meuron in their factory for Ricola, makers of herbal sweets, have been silk-screened with foliage and plant motifs to provide a leafy camouflage, reflecting the sylvan location of the works as well as the nature of the product being made there.

Since Eero Saarinen's idyllic setting for General Motors' Technical Center at Warren, Michigan, built in the early 1950s, its 36–hectare site conceived on a scale dictated by the automobile rather than by man, a pattern of luxuriance has accompanied the physical location of major industrial complexes, which, seen against the pressure for development in open countryside in densely populated parts of Europe, seems profligate. Meanwhile the trend has been for industry to leave the city, in Europe as in the USA. With neat, if unintentional irony, the site of the celebrated Citroën works at Javel in Paris is now itself a fine modern urban park.

Stockley Park is the Trafford Park of our time, sited just beyond the runways of Heathrow on a large site where only the methane pipes peeping out of the swelling hillocks of the new Country Park and golf course betray its origins as an infill site. In a setting every bit as carefully premeditated as that of the landscape garden at Stowe, linked by serpentine roads and watercourses, a series of sleek sheds by some of the best regarded British architects of the 1980s, among them Foster Associates, Ian Ritchie, Arup Associates and Eric Parry, are home to the blue-chip names of finance, IT and computer software, mostly Californian and Japanese enterprises. The ubiquitous car parks are screened by careful planting and the setting, buildings harboured by streams, lakes, mature trees, thoughtful planting and subtle contouring, demonstrates modern traditional landscape design at its best. This secure, protective environment is the twenty-first century version of the paternalistic factory village, although here the end product is information, not goods.

Cleanliness is the image of modern industry, as grime was of its predecessor. An unrelenting programme during the 1960s and '70s,

in which the buildings of the Pennine mill towns were stripped of the soot of decades, revealing their stonework blinking in the daylight, coincided with the decline of the British textile industry. There was little recognition of the importance of some of these seminal buildings. At Marshalls' Temple Mill the vast top-lit weaving shed with its ranks of glazed cupolas and Egyptian frontages disappeared in the 1960s (leaving as evidence just the office block, now the headquarters of a mail order company), hardly noticed and far less mourned than the nine parabolic roofs of the Brynmawr Rubber Plant, reduced to rubble in June 2001. Similarly, the rise of the Asian car industry has seen the dereliction and piecemeal demolition of the pioneer Detroit car factories, happily countered by the renaissance of the Fiat Lingotto, saved largely by the commitment

The campus as factory. View over the lake to General Motors HQ, Warren, Michigan, 1948–57, architect Eero Saarinen.

to its cause by the internationally respected architect Renzo Piano, who even has an office in the building.

In the 1960s came a move to present the industrial past to new generations. A network of museums now stretches from the Ironbridge Gorge (Coalbrookdale) to Lowell, Massachusetts, even involving the manufacture of authentic items, such as textiles or ceramics, before the eyes of a curious public and for the bottomless purses of the heritage market. Elsewhere the fabric of industry is being transformed, in the case of Sir Titus Salt's mill or the Baltic Flour Mills on the River Tyne at Gateshead into cavernous art gallery and installation spaces. Factories, mills and warehouses offer suitable congenial space for clubs, loft apartments, health clubs, prestige offices or, on occasion, revert to type, back into flatted factories and workspaces, the kind of low-rent premises in which good ideas have always been born.[5]

Kunsthallen Brandts Klædefabrik, Odense, Denmark, a clothing factory to arts centre conversion.

The 1940s Baltic Flour Mills warehouse, Gateshead, Tyneside, undergoing conversion to an arts centre in 2000.

Tate Modern, London, 2000, conversion of a power station to an art gallery. Architects, Herzog and de Meuron.

As Lowell or Nyköping, much later, vividly demonstrate, most locations for manufacture prove to be dramatically short-lived. The textile town was a social and economic phenomenon that expanded, peaked and crashed within a few decades, recorded only in the solid evidence of its structures and the published accounts of its many admiring visitors.

Company towns were doomed by their tight specialization. Nowhere illustrated this more vividly than the model industrial settlement built for George Pullman, the manufacturer of luxury railway carriages, a short way from the steel mills of south Chicago. After 1894 it would be chiefly remembered as the tainted site of one of the bitterest labour disputes in the history of organized labour. The parks, fine hotel, elegant shopping arcade, good quality housing, churches and schools that Solon Beman and Nathan Barrett, respectively Pullman's architect and landscape architect, had conjured up out of the prairie at astonishing speed between 1880 and 1881 could do nothing to eradicate that ugly stain.

By definition, the settings for the early stages of industrial experiment vanished as victims of their own success. The crude smelters' huts along the River Severn or the Morris garage at Cowley outside Oxford were quickly discarded in the rush to growth, as the small artisan enterprise became large scale. One mill in Coventry saw manufacture within its walls shift from cotton ribbon making to sewing machines, then to bicycles and then, logically enough, to the internal combustion engine – at which point its name became Motor Mills. Out of each slump came a new opportunity.

Heavy industry has left heavy buildings. In the Ruhr in Germany, the remarkable transformation of the landscape of the coalfields and steelworks around Duisburg came about from a determination not to obliterate the recent history and structures of the region, as it had functioned until the mid-1980s. With the closure of the Zollverein

The Industrial Museum (Museum of Work), Nyköping, Sweden, converted from a 1916 cotton mill.

Colliery in 1986, the area became a major (and, necessarily, unique) regeneration project. Although a scheme on such a scale and carried out with such vision is not replicable across other graveyards of heavy industry, it offers a seductive alternative to the more straightforward (and finite) options of the factory as museum.

The strategy at Duisburg-Nord was based upon retaining and celebrating the structures of industry and bringing the landscape to life by day and night. Much of the huge area has been adapted, rather than redesigned. The gigantic skeletons, threaded by pipes, tracks, waterways and old railway lines, and the tough, subtly replanted landscape, are left to speak for themselves. Local people, many of whom had worked there, have been involved at a practical level, suggesting the uses for structures that might otherwise have been carelessly demolished. It is the visible and honest connection of the site with its industrial origins that gives it such force and has led to it becoming the most admired post-industrial park in Europe.

The Ruhr still hard at work, seen from a post-industrial country park, Landschaft Duisburg-Nord.

Canalside in leisure use with the silhouette of the disused steelworks in the background, Landschaft Duisburg-Nord, Ruhr, 1990s. Landscape architects Annaliese and Peter Latz.

At the symbolic centre, the Piazza Metallica is designed around a 'paved' core, constructed from eroded pig-iron plates. The former blast furnaces are lit in a blaze of celebratory colour by night, and provide climbing walls by day. Bunker gardens are hidden behind the massive walls of demolished structures. The gasometer has become a diving tank and the heavily polluted landscape is being allowed to recover through a strategy in which 'the rules of ecology [are] managed by technology', as the landscape architects Peter and Anneliese Latz put it.[6] The huge skeletons of pulleys, interspersed among a new heathland of birch trees and rough ground, are reminders that this is a landscape in remission. Coal tar lakes, mine shafts, massive pollution of both ground and water systems are the poisonous, long-term legacy of a vast dead industrial enterprise.

The triumphant reworking of the site is to celebrate, not negate, the working lives of many thousands of people, to commemorate the place in a way that changes the emphasis but consolidates memories. This complex park, serving a much shrunken but still

Landschaft Duisburg-Nord, Ruhr, 1990s. Nature reasserts its hold on a redundant steelworks.

An industrial building at a former steelworks displaying a frieze of photographs by Bernd and Hilla Becher, Landschaft Duisburg-Nord.

An early 1900s flour mill in Girona, Spain, converted to *El Punt* newspaper offices in 1999, architect Rafael Masoí Valenti.

considerable local population, provides an extraordinary range of activities, pleasures and entertainments ranging from the physically gruelling to the peaceful and contemplative.

In much of the former South Yorkshire coalfield the opposite approach has been adopted, and almost every trace of former activity erased as if to wipe away memories of mining and the bitter disputes that hastened its end. The 'new' landscape consists of eerie facsimiles of land forms, empty dual carriageways and speculatively built factories, many un-let.

More positively, the massive steel-making sheds at Temple-borough, near Rotherham, have survived to be transformed by Wilkinson Eyre into the Magna project, an ambitious, Lottery-funded science centre and winner of the Stirling Prize for 2001. The scale of the building allows the shed to remain empty like an immense carapace, within the dense blackness of which the visitor is guided through a succession of interactive science displays, each in a separate illuminated bubble or cocoon. Only with the deafening roar of the sound and light show, demonstrating the firing of the blast furnaces, comes the forcible, and necessary, reminder of the original purpose of the building. Yet like a coal-effect gas fire, it is just a symbol.

Cleaned of detritus and grime, odourless and dust free, its working parts left as sculptural objects in the space inside and out, the Templeborough Mill has become an object almost entirely out of its context – perhaps an apt enough metaphor in Britain, the birthplace of the Industrial Revolution, which now (in 2002) obtains just one fifth of its GNP from manufacturing industry. The only link back to the former working life of the area lies in the cluster of small engineering works that loiter nearby. Each specializes in some component required by manufacturing and heavy engineering industry; they survive productively in a huddle of serviceable, rough-and-ready sheds, like awkward country cousins to the huge, sophisticated black

building along the road, which once provided their raw material but now can only commemorate the making of steel with theatrical enactment of the process.

The working modern factory, landscaped politely into the background, has become almost obsequious. But as if to answer a sense of growing disquiet with this anonymity, this sense of distance, some new industrial architecture evokes the era of romantic transparency and brilliance, when gas lights blazed in the valleys and Moderne factories on the new arterial roads offered a light show after dark. A cast glass street front on a warehouse for Braun at Marktheidenfeld by Schneider and Schumacher encourages a shimmer of colour from the domestic electrical goods piled within, while the glazed front elevation of Henning Larsen's factory for Mekoprint

The steel-making sheds at Templeborough, now converted to the Magna science centre, architects Wilkinson Eyre.

in Denmark ingeniously uses a serigraph of a circuit board (one of the company's products) as solar screen by day and an emblematic motif by night. Nicholas Grimshaw's works for BMW Rolls-Royce at Goodwood in West Sussex has a 'living green roof', is sunk tactfully into gravel workings and designed into near invisibility in the precious landscape around the South Downs, but for those who penetrate this disguise and manage to find their way on to the site, the production line will be fully visible from the glazed central courtyard.

Manufacturing industry, with robotics and laser-operated and computer-programmed machinery, operates in unrelentingly clean, even sterile, windowless conditions. There may be less manufacturing in sum, but the products being made are more refined, higher value items. In its own way the age of Information Technology is as hungry for gadgets as was the era of the Industrial Revolution. The profiled steel and glass panelled sheds that typify the anonymity and slickness of nameless industrial-scale operations, whether chip assembly or car plants, call centres or research and development laboratories for biotech or electronics multinationals, form the invisible background to our lives. Un-peopled, they flash by on hoardings and posters, as backdrops to advertisements in the press and television, or, in reality, on the sites to which they have been banished, far from town. In Silicon Valley, Fen or Glen they sit, shiny, self-sufficient and purposefully secretive.

The imagery of the modern factory – however we define it – is essentially hermetic, with no references given or even hinted at. The journey from those belching furnaces reflected in the River Severn at Coalbrookdale that provoked such wonder and fear to this curious anomie has been travelled at breakneck speed. Where next?

Clean, automized assembly. The Volkswagen 'Transparent Factory' near Dresden, 1999–2001, architects–engineers, Henn Architects.

References

Preface

1 *Hell / Dante Alighieri*, ed. Steve Ellis (London, 1994).
2 Peter Buchanan, 'Reviving Lingotto', *Architectural Review*, CC/11 (1996), pp. 62–7.

1 Factory as Image

1 Francis Spufford, *I May be Some Time* (London, 1996), p. 40. Thomas Carlyle, who knew Manchester in the 1830s from his study of Chartism, chose a very similar metaphor when he compared the sound of the pounding mill machinery to 'the boom of an Atlantic tide . . . sublime as a Niagara, or more so'.
2 The others had been for John Wilkinson's Coalbrookdale forge and for Coates's and Jarrett's oil mill in Kingston upon Hull. John Mosse, 'The Albion Mills 1784–1791', *Transactions of the Newcomen Society*, XL (1967–8), pp. 47–54.
3 *Ibid.*
4 Robert Barker's and Frederick Birnie's panorama of London from the south bank of the Thames was drawn in the winter of 1790–91 from the roof of the Albion Mill. Thomas Girtin's version, of 1797–8, was taken from the west side of Albion Place and therefore showed the gaunt skeleton of the mill in the foreground. *Panoramania!*, exh. cat., Barbican Art Gallery, London (1988).
5 Adrian Forty, *Words and Buildings: A Vocabulary of Modern Architecture* (London, 2000), pp. 188–92.
6 Stephen Daniels, *Humphry Repton* (New Haven and London, 1999), pp. 247–50.
7 R. Offor, *The Papers of Benjamin Gott* (1931), p. 182.
8 'The Gott Papers', *Thoresby Society*, XXXII [Leeds] (1931), p. 241.
9 Karl Friedrich Schinkel, *The English Journey*, ed. D. Bindman and G. Riemann (New Haven and London, 1993), p. 4.
10 *Ibid.*, p. 208, note 546. See also Adriaan Linters, *Industria: Industrial Architecture in Belgium* (Liège, 1986).

11 Arnold Bennett describes the processes within a 'model three-oven bank' at a small pottery employing around 100 workers in his novel *Anna of the Five Towns* (1902).

12 Essay by Hans-Ulrich Kilian in Kurt Ackermann, *Building for Industry* (Godalming, 1991), pp. 30–31.

13 John Evelyn was concerned by the smoke levels of seventeenth-century London, and wrote *Fumifugium* (1661) to argue his case, which was supported by King Charles II. It is still in print, reissued by the National Society for Clean Air.

14 Jenny Uglow, *Elizabeth Gaskell* (London, 1993).

15 Anthony Beever, *Stalingrad* (London, 1998), pp. 393–4, quoting Alexander Werth. The major, but inconclusive, attack on the Tractor Factory was undertaken between 9 and 12 October 1942.

2 Factory as Model: Early Versions

1 Thomas Markus, *Buildings & Power* (London, 1993), p. 250.

2 Arthur Young, *Travels in France during the Years 1787, 1788 & 1789*, ed. Constantia Maxwell (Cambridge, 1929), p. 199. Wilkinson's brother John sat at an iron desk and planned to be buried in a cast-iron coffin.

3 Bernard Clement, 'Le Creusot: From Foundry to Town', *Rassegna*, XIX, 70 – 1997/ II (Company Towns issue).

4 Anthony Vidler, *Claude-Nicolas Ledoux* (Cambridge, MA, and London, 1990), p. 75. See also my Chapter 3.

5 Claude-Nicolas Ledoux, *L'Architecture considerée sous le rapport de l'art, des moeurs et de la législation* (1804).

6 James Nasmyth, *Autobiography*, ed. Samuel Smiles (1883), is quoted as having 'rarely seen a more faithful and zealous set of workmen'.

7 Simon Sebag Montefiore, *The Life of Potemkin* (London, 2000), p. 301.

8 Ian Christie, *The Benthams in Russia, 1780–1791* (Oxford, 1993), pp. 177–8.

9 For two accounts of Samuel Bentham's efforts, see *Mechanics Magazine* (13 March 1849), pp. 294–9, and *Civil Engineer and Architects Journal*, XIV (1853), p. 453.

10 Sidney Pollard, *The Genesis of Modern Management* (London, 1965).

11 Ian Donnachie and George Hewitt, *Historic New Lanark* (Edinburgh, 1993).

12 Gregory Claeys, ed., *Selected Works of Robert Owen*, vol. I (London, 1993).

13 Gillian Darley, *Villages of Vision* (London, 1975), p. 81.

14 Southey speculated that Owen had been influenced by Moravian settlements. The community had established Fairfield, at Droylsden outside Manchester, as a self-sufficient village in 1785, and Owen, like Dale, must have known of the progressive, if religious, experiment.

15 Dolores Hayden, *Seven Communitarian Experiments* (Cambridge, MA, and London, 1976); also Gillian Darley, 'The Moravians: Building for a Higher Purpose', *Architectural Review*, CLXXVII (April 1985), pp. 45–9.

16 Thomas Bender, *Towards an Urban Vision* (Baltimore and London, 1975), p. 23.

17 Bender, *Towards an Urban Vision*, p. 28.

18 Anthony Trollope, *North America* (London, 1986), I, p. 254.

19 Spiro Kostoff, *The City Shaped* (London, 1991), p. 169.

20 Markus, *Buildings & Power*, p. 299, quoting from Godin's publication of 1871.

21 William Jolly, *W. H. Lever* (London, 1976).

22 Polly Toynbee's *A Working Life* (London, 1971) recounts her harsh experiences there. In *Hard Work* (London, 2003) she returns to find a smaller workforce and improved conditions.

3 Modern Models

1 Robert Beevers, *The Garden City Utopia: A Critical Biography of Ebenezer Howard* (New York, 1988), pp. 7–8, quoting Howard's words in the mid-1920s.

2 Mervyn Miller, *Letchworth: The First Garden City* (Chichester, 1989), p. 145.

3 Nikolaus Pevsner and Edward Hubbard, *Buildings of England: South Lancashire* (London, 1969), p. 405: 'The area is very large; the architecture, however, calls for no comments . . .'. Although Trafford Park is generally credited with being the world's first industrial estate, the Scottish Co-operative Workers' Society set one up at Shieldhall in 1887. See Michael Stratton and Barrie Trinder, *Twentieth Century Industrial Archaeology* (London, 2000).

4 Carroll Pursell, *The Machine in America* (Baltimore and London, 1995), pp. 210–13; also by the same author, *White Heat* (London, 1994), especially chap. 4.

5 Pursell, *White Heat*, p. 115.

6 Jean-Louis Cohen, *Scenes of the World to Come: European Architecture and the American Challenge, 1893–1960*, exh. cat., Canadian Centre for Architecture, Montreal (1995), p. 80.

7 Andrew Saint, *Image of the Architect* (New Haven and London, 1983), p. 80, note.

8 Brian Carter, ed., *Albert Kahn: Inspiration for the Modern*, exh. cat., University of Michigan Museum of Art, Ann Arbor (2001), pp. 48–9.

9 Jean-Louis Cohen, 'Zlin: An Industrial Republic', *Rassegna*, XIX, 70 – 1997/ II (Company Towns issue), pp. 42–5. Also Jane Pavitt, 'The Bata Project: A Social and Industrial Experiment', *Journal of the Twentieth Century Society*, I: *Industrial Architecture* (Summer 1994), chap. 9.

10 Pavitt, 'The Bata Project', p. 36.

11 Thomas Bata, *How I Began* (East Tilbury, 1934).

12 See *Zlín*, exhibition catalogue, Le Creusot Montceau (2002), pp. 70–77

13 Pavitt, 'The Bata Project'.

14 Jolyon Drury and Derek Sugden, 'Briefing: Factories', *Architectural Design*, XLIX/2 (1974), pp. 92–4.

15 Victoria Perry, *Built for a Better Future: The Brynmawr Rubber Factory* (Oxford, 1994); see p. 11, foreword by Andrew Saint.

16 Perry, *Built for a Better Future*, pp. 29–30.

17 Ironically enough, the towers, although ruined and periodically threatened with demolition, have outlived the Brynmawr factory.
18 Perry, *Built for a Better Future*, p. 56.
19 Elain Harwood, '"Prestige Pancakes": The Influence of American Planning in British Industry since the War', *Journal of the Twentieth Century Society*, I: *Industrial Architecture* (Summer 1994), chap. 4.
20 Leland Roth, *American Architecture* (Boulder, CO, 2000), pp. 543–5; see also Balthazar Korab, *Columbus, Indiana* (Kalamazoo, MI, 1989).
21 The Darlington plant was for sale and sadly run down by 1998; see *Architectural Review*, CCIV (November 1998), p. 18. See also Elain Harwood, *England: A Guide to Post-war Listed Buildings* (London, 2000), no. 1.84.
22 Deyan Sudjic, 'Six Factories, One Design, No Dogma', *Design*, 387 (March 1981), pp. 54–5.
23 Martin Pawley, *Terminal Architecture* (London, 1998), p. 184.

4 Factory as Innovator

1 Cited in P. Morton Shand, 'Iron and Steel', *Architectural Review*, LXXII (November 1932), p. 169.
2 Cited in Markus, *Buildings & Power*, p. 263.
3 Markus, *Buildings & Power*.
4 Etruria was designed by Joseph Pickford, a local architect working to a detailed brief and plan provided by Wedgwood and his business partner Thomas Bentley. See *Wedgwood of Etruria and Barlaston*, exh. cat., City Museum and Art Gallery, Hanley (1980).
5 Pollard, *Genesis of Modern Management*, p. 304.
6 R.J.M. Sutherland, ed., *Structural Iron, 1750–1850*, Studies in the History of Civil Engineering, IX (Aldershot, 1997), especially chap. 2.
7 Jenny Uglow, *The Lunar Men: The Friends Who Made the Future* (London, 2002), is an illuminating account of these interconnections.
8 Markus, *Buildings & Power*, p. 125.
9 Sutherland, *Structural Iron*, Introduction.
10 John Newman, *Buildings of England: North East and East Kent* (London, 1976), p. 453.
11 Especially by Sigfried Giedion in *Space Time and Architecture* (Cambridge, MA, and London, 1941).
12 A. W. Skempton, 'The Boat Store, Sheerness and its Place in Structural History', in *Structural Iron and Steel, 1850–1900*, ed. Robert Thorne, Studies in the History of Civil Engineering, X (Aldershot, 2000).
13 Fairbairn's memoirs, completed by N. Pole, were published in 1877.
14 Peter Collins, *Concrete* (London, 1959).
15 David P. Billington, *Robert Maillart and the Art of Reinforced Concrete* (Cambridge,

MA, and London, 1990), pp. 13–18.

16 David Billington, *Maillart* (Cambridge, 1997). Maillart's firm built numerous reinforced concrete factories in Russia and the Baltic States from 1912 onwards; they included a rubber factory at Riga, a steel mill in Kamemskaya, a cold store in St Petersburg and, largest of all, the Kharkov factory for GEC of Russia – a massive enterprise involving 1,000 concrete workers and engineers. By October 1916 the job was complete; by the time of his forced departure a few months later, he had lost everything.

17 Florence Dempsey, 'Nela Park', *Architectural Record*, XXXV/6 (June 1914), pp. 469–504.

18 Federico Bucci, *Albert Kahn* (Princeton, NJ, 1993), pp. 37–8; also Grant Hildebrand, 'Beautiful Factories', in *Albert Kahn: Inspiration for the Modern*, ed. Brian Carter, exh. cat., University of Michigan Museum of Art, Ann Arbor (2001).

19 Peter Collins, *Concrete* (London, 1959), p. 235.

20 Gavin Stamp, ed., *Sir Owen Williams, 1890–1969*, exh. cat., Architectural Association, London (1986). The comment is from Frank Newby's piece on Williams.

21 In W. J. Cameron, *A Series of Talks* (Dearborn, MI, 1937).

22 The famous glazed diagonal conveyor belts were added the following year, a reminder of the criss-crossed conveyors that Charles Sheeler celebrated in one of his photographs of 1927 of the Ford Rouge Plant.

23 Until 2000 the company organized regular tours within their public relations programme; these have been cancelled as an economy measure – somewhat shortsightedly it might seem, viewed against the efficacy of such publicity.

24 For a full discussion of this, see Joel Davidson, 'Building for War, Preparing for Peace', in *World War II and the American Dream*, exh. cat., National Building Museum, Washington, DC (1994). See also Martin Pawley, *Theory and Design in the Second Machine Age* (London, 1990), chap. 6.

25 Kenneth Frampton, *Modern Architecture: A Critical History* (London, 1992), p. 231.

26 *Architectural Review*, CXVI (1954), pp. 9–19.

27 Chris Wilkinson, *Supersheds*, 2nd edn (London, 1996), p. 50.

28 *Ibid.*, p. 66.

29 Anthony Hunt, 'The Future', in Wilkinson, *Supersheds*, p. 152.

30 *Architects' Journal* (29 July 1999), pp. 33–7.

5 Factory as Icon

1 Le Corbusier, *Towards a New Architecture* (London, 1927), p. 41.

2 A point illustrated with three photographs, the Val Nelle factory, 1928–30, and the Kolb soap factory in Zurich by Kellermüller & Hofmann and the Königsgrube Mine Works at Bochum by Theodor Merrill, both of 1930.

3 Reyner Banham, *Theory and Design in the First Machine Age* (London, 1960) emphazises how the modernist agenda was already intact in the pre-war writings of the Futurists, but shorn of any pretensions to social purpose.

4 Jean-Louis Cohen, *Scenes of the World to Come: European Architecture and the American Challenge, 1893–1960* (Paris, 1995), pp. 63–8.

5 H.-R. Hitchcock and Philip Johnson, *The International Style* (New York, 1932), p. 44.

6 Annemarie Jaeggi, *Fagus: Industrial Culture from Werkbund to Bauhaus* (New York, 2000), p. 86.

7 Stanford Anderson, *Peter Behrens and a New Architecture for the Twentieth Century* (Cambridge, MA, and London), chap. 7 on AEG. Later, between 1929 and 1938, Behrens designed the Linz state tobacco factory, a banded and curved six-storey steel-framed building with continuous strip windows.

8 Jaeggi, *Fagus*, p. 7.

9 Reyner Banham, 'The Glass Paradise', *Architectural Review*, CXXV (February 1959), pp. 87–9; see also his *Concrete Atlantis* (Cambridge, MA, and London, 1986).

10 Later in his working life, Poelzig carried out a huge project for I. G. Farben, under the aegis of Albert Speer.

11 Oskar Beyer, ed., *Eric Mendelsohn: Letters of an Architect* (London, New York and Toronto, 1967), p. 46.

12 Regina Stephan, ed., *Erich Mendelsohn, Architect, 1887–1953* (New York, 1999), pp. 65–6.

13 Banham, *Concrete Atlantis*, p. 6.

14 Forty, *Words and Buildings*, p. 184.

15 William C. Brumfield, ed., *Reshaping Russian Architecture* (Cambridge, 1990).

16 Cass Gilbert, designer of a flamboyant Gothic skyscraper for Woolworth in Manhattan, had built a US Army Supply base in Brooklyn in 1918.

17 Murray Fraser, 'Eero Saarinen and the Boundaries of Technology', *The Oxford Review of Architecture*, 1 (1996), p. 59.

6 Factory as Sales Tool

1 Howard Colvin, *A Biographical Dictionary of British Architects, 1600–1840*, 3rd edn (New Haven and London, 1995), p. 142, note correcting the dates given in *Architectural Review*, CXXVII (1960), pp. 280–82.

2 W. G. Rimmer, *Marshalls of Leeds* (Cambridge, 1960).

3 *The Penny Magazine*, XII (30 December 1843), pp. 501–8.

4 *Inspiration of Egypt*, exh. cat., Brighton Museum (1983).

5 Benjamin Disraeli, *Sybil* (Oxford, 1970), pp. 183–5. Disraeli also added that Mr Trafford had built them a model village, supplied with gardens, schools, public baths and church, paid them well and gave them a half-day on which they could go to market.

6 Cited in Andor Gomme and David Walker, *The Architecture of Glasgow* (London, 1968), p. 226.

7 Jaeggi, *Fagus*, p. 41.

8 Paul Collins and Michael Stratton, *British Car Factories from 1896* (Godmanstone, Dorset, 1993). The founder died in 1914 and at the outbreak of war the building became a munitions factory. It remained a defence establishment until the 1970s.

9 Vicky Richardson, 'Production Line', *RIBA Journal*, CVII (July 2000), pp. 36–42.

10 *Les Usines Citroën*, exhibition at Bibliothèque des Arts Decorative, Paris, 1999. In the early 1920s the thrilling potential offered by cheap automobile manufacture inspired Le Corbusier to call his prototype house for mass production the Citrohan.

11 David L. Lewis, *The Public Image of Henry Ford* (Detroit, 1976).

12 Grant Hildebrand, 'Beautiful Factories', in *Albert Kahn: Inspiration for the Modern*, ed. Brian Carter, exh. cat., University of Michigan Museum of Art, Ann Arbor (2001).

13 Jaeggi, *Fagus*, see chapter on Fagus and Photography. Renger-Patzsch was commissioned to take another series of photographs in 1952, presumably to record how the plant had fared during the war.

14 Julian Holder, 'Reflecting Change: Pilkington as a Patron of Modern Architecture and Design', *Journal of the Twentieth Century Society*, I: *Industrial Architecture* (Summer 1994), chap. 7. Maxwell Fry built a glass tower block as their headquarters building at St Helens in 1953.

15 Joan S. Skinner, *Form and Fancy: Factories and Factory Buildings by Wallis, Gilbert & Partners* (Liverpool, 1997).

16 Gavin Weightman, *The Making of Modern London* (London, 1984), p. 59.

17 Skinner, *Form and Fancy*, p. 125.

18 Brian Carter, *Johnson Wax Administration Building and Research Tower* (London, 1998), p. 22, quotation from Sam Johnson.

19 Frank Lloyd Wright, *Autobiography* (London, 1945), p. 408.

20 Rowan Moore, ed., *Structure, Space and Skin: The Work of Nicholas Grimshaw & Partners* (London, 1993), pp. 158–75.

21 Jonathan Glancey, 'Dream Factory', *The Guardian* (7 January 2002).

7 Factory as Laboratory or Laboratory as Factory?

1 Harry Miller, *Halls of Dartford, 1785–1985* (London, 1985).

2 Naomi Klein, *No Logo* (London, 2000), p. xvi.

3 Kyung Park, 'Inner City Borders in Detroit', *Architectural Design*, LXIX/7–8 (1999), pp. 80–81.

4 *Architects' Journal*, CCXVI (31 October 2002).

5 James Nasmyth, inventor of the steam hammer, began his business in just such a building, which he illustrated fondly in his autobiography. The Greater London Council commissioned Yorke Rosenberg & Mardall to build the Ada Street Workshops in Hackney in 1965–6; see Elizabeth Robinson, *Twentieth Century Buildings in Hackney* (London, 1999).

6 In *Topos* [Munich], 26 (1999), special issue.

Select Bibliography

Ackermann, Kurt, *Building for Industry* (Godalming, 1991) (German original)
Banham, Reyner, *Theory and Design in the First Machine Age* (London, 1960)
—, *A Concrete Atlantis: US Industrial Building and European Modern Architecture, 1900–1925* (Cambridge, MA, and London, 1986)
Bindman, David, and Gottfried Riemann, eds, *Karl Friedrich Schinkel: 'The English Journey'* (New Haven and London, 1993)
Brumfield, William C., ed., *Reshaping Russian Architecture* (Cambridge, 1990)
Bucci, Federico, *Albert Kahn, Architect of Ford* (New York, 1993) (French original)
Cohen, Jean-Louis, *Scenes of the World to Come: European Architecture and the American Challenge, 1893–1960* (Paris, 1995)
Ferrier, Jacques, *Usines*, 2 vols (Paris, 1987–91)
Frampton, Kenneth, *Modern Architecture: A Critical History*, 3rd edn (London, 1992)
Giedion, Sigfried, *Mechanization Takes Command* (New York, 1948)
Journal of the Twentieth Century Society, 1: *Industrial Architecture Special Issue* (London, 1994)
Jaeggi, Annemarie, *Fagus: Industrial Culture from Werkbund to Bauhaus* (New York, 2000) (German original, 1998)
Kahn, Moritz, *The Design and Construction of Industrial Buildings* (London, 1917)
Klingender, Francis D., *Art and the Industrial Revolution*, rev. edn (London, 1968)
Le Corbusier, *Towards a New Architecture* (London, 1927) (French original)
Markus, Thomas, *Buildings & Power* (London, 1993)
Pawley, Martin, *Theory and Design in the Second Machine Age* (Oxford, 1990)
Rassegna, XIX, 70 – 1997/ II (Company Towns issue)
Wilkinson, Chris, *Supersheds*, 2nd edn (Oxford, 1996)
Winter, John, *Industrial Architecture: A Survey of Factory Building* (London, 1970)

Photographic Acknowledgements

The author and publishers wish to express their thanks to the following sources of illustrative material and/or permission to reproduce it: Photos Aerofilms.com: p. 71; photo Architects Co-Partnership, courtesy of Alan Powers: p. 99; photo © courtesy of BALTIC Centre for Contemporary Art, Gateshead: p. 201 (top); Berlinische Galerie Berlin (Landesmuseum für moderne Kunst, Photographie und Architektur): p. 38; The Boots Company Archive: pp. 124, 125; photo Cadbury Trebor Bassett: p. 69; photo courtesy of Coop Himmelblau: p. 186; photo Cyfarthfa Castle Museum & Art Gallery, Merthyr Tydfil: p. 27; photos Gillian Darley: pp. 68, 111, 177; courtesy of Gillian Darley: pp. 58, 66 (top), 73, 137; Deutsches Technikmuseum Berlin (Archiv der A. Borsigschen Vermögensverwaltung Berlin), on long-term loan to the Stadtsmuseum, Berlin; photo Deutsches Technikmuseum Berlin: p. 34; photos © Edifice/Darley: pp. 11, 22, 43 (left), 47, 48, 49, 56, 63, 113, 126, 127, 135, 142, 144, 173, 176, 182, 183, 185 (top), 196, 203, 204, 205, 206, 207, 209; © Edifice/Hart-Davis: p. 24 (foot); © Edifice/Lewis: pp. 43 (right), 61, 78, 81, 110, 164, 165, 179; © Edifice/Worpole: pp. 174, 188; photos Norman Foster (courtesy of Foster and Partners): pp. 132, 184; photo Guildhall Library, London, © Corporation of London: p. 19; photo courtesy of Jernkontoret, Stockholm: p. 16; photos © Joe Kerr: pp. 180, 199; photo courtesy of Kunsthallen Brandts Klædefabrik, Odense: p. 200; photos Leeds Local Studies Library, © Leeds Library and Information Services: pp. 159, 160, 161; photos courtesy of Philippa Lewis p. 191; photos Library of Congress (Prints & Photographs Division): pp. 55 (HABS [NY,11-NELEB.v,40-3]), 83 [left] (LC-D4-500948), 83 [right] (LC-D4-72249); (FSA-OWI Collection), photos Alfred T. Palmer: pp. 88 (LC-USE6-D-000764), 89 (LC-USE6-D-000774); Musée Constantin Meunier, Brussels (Musées Royaux des Beaux-Arts de Belgique)/photo © IRPA/KIK, Bruxelles: p. 10; photos © Crown copyright/National Monument Record: pp. 66 (foot), 102; Oak Spring Garden Library, Upperville, VA (Coll. Mrs Paul Mellon), photo courtesy of Mrs Paul Mellon: p. 24 (top); photo courtesy of Richard Rogers Partnership: p. 133; photo Crown Copyright RCAHM: p. 167; William Salt Library, Stafford/photo Staffordshire Record Office: p. 107; Amoret Tanner Collection: p. 158 (foot); photo courtesy of Valode & Pistre: p. 185 (foot); photos courtesy of Volkswagen AG: pp. 189, 211; photo William F. Winter, Jr.: p. 55; photo: Gerald Zugmann: p. 186.

Index